TREK

TREK

*An American Woman, Two Small Children,
and Survival in World War II Germany*

Mary Hunt Jentsch

Foreword and Epilogue by Steve Mumford

McWitty Press
New York, New York

Library of Congress Cataloging-in-Publication Data
Jentsch, Mary Hunt, 1898-1972.
Trek : an American woman, two small children and survival in World War II
Germany / by Mary Hunt Jentsch ; foreword and epilogue by Steve Mumford.
    p. cm.
ISBN-13: 978-0-9755618-5-0 (pbk. : alk. paper)
ISBN-10: 0-9755618-5-5 (pbk. : alk. paper)
1. Jentsch, Mary Hunt, 1898-1972. 2. World War, 1939-1945--Personal
narratives, American. 3. Americans--Germany--Biography. 4. Women--
United States--Biography. I. Title.
    D811.5.J3775 2008d
    940.53'161092--dc22
    [B]
                            2008027957

Printed in the United States of America
First Edition

Trek is an account of World War II and of what happened to ordinary people in villages of northeast Germany. When Russian troops crossed the border into East Prussia in January 1945, millions of desperate Germans fled their homes in "treks"—on foot, in horse-drawn wagons, and on bicycles—carrying the few possessions they could. That invasion was the end of a united Germany, splitting it into East and West for almost fifty years. It was also the end of a family, which, like Germany itself, the war had cut in two.

Contents

Foreword

I ALWAYS LOOKED FORWARD to visits from my maternal grandmother, Mary Hunt Jentsch, the author of this book. Gran, born in 1898 in Louisville, Kentucky, grew up in an era of the mighty Mississippi and its riverboats.

She was a gifted storyteller, as you will soon discover, and I was held rapt by her tales. She disliked sentimentality and appreciated a story with an edge—like the tales of the Brothers Grimm, with their supernatural beings and glimpses into the dark corners of the human psyche. I think she often melded these stories into her own.

Gran told me stories about her childhood and of Katy, the "Negro" nanny who helped raise her. She talked of the Mississippi and often sang lullabies and folk songs to me, like "Oh, Susannah." Gran wasn't snobbish about class or ethnicity, but she gravitated toward fellow travelers, to minds that sparked with imagination and generosity. She could forgive and even enjoy mad irrationality, but never obtuseness. I suspect that her intelligent, sociable nature was a key to her surviving the war.

My grandmother wrote the manuscript for *Trek* in 1959, and it was passed around among family members. As a teenager, obsessed with comic books and cars, I had no interest in reading her story, carefully typewritten on onion-skin paper, safely stored in its own dog-eared cardboard box.

Reading it now, I find it embodies the qualities I loved in Gran: witty and spirited, but also unsentimental and frank.

The Beginning

MARY HUNT FIRST ARRIVED in Boston to attend Simmons College in 1918, the year World War I ended. She had an adventurous streak; she was a romantic who filled her scrapbook with poetry and theater programs from the plays that she loved. Years later she shared this passion with my mother, Erika, and passed along a hopeless infatuation with Laurence Olivier. Leaving college, she took a job at Houghton Mifflin reading manuscripts.

One of her co-workers was Esther Forbes, who later won a Pulitzer Prize for her biography of Paul Revere and whose book *Johnny Tremain*, a story of the American Revolution written for young adults, is still a classic. Esther and Mary became close friends, joined by another Mary—Mary Allen, a Bryn Mawr graduate and world traveler who had been an ambulance driver in France and Germany during the Great War. Through them, Mary Hunt was drawn into a sophisticated world of people from many different backgrounds and countries.

At a party they gave, one of the guests was a young man named Gerhart Jentsch, a German who had come to Harvard in 1921 as a doctoral student in Economics. In a burst of patriotic fervor, Mary refused to meet him, announcing that she would stay in her room because, "I'm not going to eat with any Hun."

Eventually they did meet and gradually fell in love. Her initial refusal became a lovers' joke. There is a picture Gerhart gave her, he in profile, elegant and romantic, and on the back in German he wrote: "I hope that everyone in America is not like you, so that one day I will be able to accept the invitation to return."

Gerhart's family was of limited means but his father, a retired superintendent of schools in Silesia, put a high value on education. Gerhart and his two brothers all attended university, and Gerhart, after leaving Harvard to finish his doctoral degree in Paris, set up an international student exchange program there with his friend, John Rothschild.

Mary also left Boston for Paris. In 1926, she sailed to France to marry the man she had once refused to dine with. "I landed on Friday, and we were married on the following Tuesday, January 26," she wrote to her friend Esther. "In France one can be married only on Tuesdays and Saturdays....Guess who my witness was—Dulles!

"Early Tuesday morning I put on my dark green wedding dress and Gerhart's violets and off we sailed with our witnesses to the mairie *(town hall) near the Pantheon. We were the first to be married – about nine-thirty and it was quite quaint and beautifully simple. There were three other couples in a Renaissance-looking room lighted by candles. We signed our names in innumerable books and then the* Maire *(mayor) came in in a flowing robe; the clerk read our names and the* Maire *read us the French marriage laws, and pronounced us man and wife.*

"He also presented us with a marriage book with the law printed out, and our names and dates, and space for fourteen children (God forbid) and a treatise on the care and feeding of same. When a French girl marries she loses all her rights and becomes a minor, so G. had the lawyer draw up a marriage contract by which I keep all my rights, 'according to the law of the state of Kentucky,' so we have innumerable documents with our signatures in dozens of places. After the ceremony, at

about 10, we three—Dulles* and my husband and I—strolled across the street to the Luxemburg Gardens and meandered about in a dazed way, watching the children roll their hoops, drinking in the delicious spring air and grinning fatuously at the stone lions."

Through her husband's exchange program, Mary met young people from all over the world. She thought they were "really fine, most of them, and all young, and it makes me feel as if there really is a future for the world."

After almost ten years in Paris, Gerhart and John Rothschild moved the exchange program to Geneva, Switzerland, site of the League of Nations and an important diplomatic and cultural center. There in 1935, Mary and Gerhart's first child, Erika, my mother, was born. The economic depression and the threat of war had put severe strains on the student exchange program and by 1936, Gerhart was teaching International Organization at the Geneva College of Women, an affiliate of Mount Holyoke College in Massachusetts. In 1938, my uncle, Jerry, was born in Geneva.

Gerhart was offered a post at several American universities to work as an assistant professor. Instead, he took a job with the Institute for Foreign Policy Research, the Reich's Foreign Office, directing the "America department."

In January 1940, the couple moved to Berlin.

In retrospect, knowing what lay ahead, it's hard to understand how Gerhart and Mary could have made such a move. Part of the reason was financial. Hitler's moves into

---

*Eleanor Lansing Dulles was the sister of John Foster Dulles, the Secretary of State under President Eisenhower, and Allen Dulles, director of the CIA in the same administration. She went on to become a member of the U.S. State Department as an expert on Germany.

Austria, the Sudetenland, and Czechoslovakia had put a severe strain on Gerhart's position and that of other Germans in Switzerland and the U.S.

Mary, writing to her friend Mary Allen in November, 1939—two months after Hitler had invaded Poland, and Britain and France had declared war—tried to explain Gerhart's decision to return to Germany and take the job at the Institute for Foreign Policy Research, as well as her own decision to accompany him.

"I don't see anything to do but go. First, I would not like to be separated from G—and certainly he could not go to U.S.A. and even if he wanted to go could not get a job. Secondly, he couldn't send us money from Germany, and I really don't see how we would live, and I would not want to sponge even if my friends and family could afford it, which nobody can anymore. Also, I would be very uncomfortable there as the wife of a German. And finally, I believe things over here look blacker to you in America and while no country in a state of war is pleasant to live in, I don't think it's as bad as you think."

Gerhart's friend and former partner, John Rothschild, also tried to explain and defend the couple's decision in a December, 1939 letter to Eleanor Dulles:

"1. Gerhart has been outspokenly critical of some of the Reich's internal policies, notably the treatment of Jews. I owe to him some very interesting bits of information on this score, which are decidedly hostile to the regime.

"2. His indignation against the invasion of Czechoslovakia was as intense and forthright as anything I have heard on the subject.

"3. He is not anti-British or anti-French.

"*4. He hates power politics no matter who plays them.*

"*5. His central interest continues to be a harmonious integration of Europe.*

"*6. He feels himself German, just as you and I feel ourselves to be American.*"

He added: "I am sure that Gerhart is not going back to Germany to help Hitler win the war or to fortify Hitlerism. Had it occurred to you that he may be going back to help bring about changes in internal and foreign policy?"

Mary Hunt Jentsch sent a final letter to Mary Allen, dated February 6, 1940, just before the war arrived. It tells of the 27-hour trip from Geneva to Berlin on darkened trains, past darkened stations, through a countryside where no lights showed. The children, she wrote, had gotten sick, but in Berlin they were living in a pension while looking for an apartment. She reports that she was able to find oranges, apples, and milk, though no coffee. She mentions an organization she had heard about in New York that will purchase supplies in a neutral country and send them on to Germany. Her list of things she needs, in order of descending urgency, begins with soap flakes and ends with Vicks salve.

After that, as far as her friends and family were concerned, Mary Hunt Jentsch vanished. She was caught with her two small children on the wrong side of the battle line and was not heard from again until 1945.

Steve Mumford
—New York City, 2008

Chapter One

SILESIA
1940 to 1942
The Last Days of Traditional Life

ARRIVING IN GERMANY IN JANUARY 1940, Mary and Gerhart Jentsch found an apartment in Berlin. Almost immediately the British began their night bombing. In the summer, Mary left Berlin with Erika and Jerry for the countryside of Silesia to stay with Gerhart's parents, Erdman and Hedwig Jentsch, at their home in Langenbielau. Mary begins her story there, in a world that had remained the same for several hundred years—and was about to vanish.

> "...a good league hence
> Underneath the mountain
> Right against the forest fence..."
> lyrics from "Good King Wenceslas"

There is no fairer land than Silesia—the part I know best. Southwest of the beautiful old city of Breslau-on-the-Oder, that southeastern outpost of the Hanseatic League, the forested Eulengebirge (Owl Mountains) with their sparkling streams tumbling into fertile valleys. Not impressive mountains, but intimate and enticing.

The little valleys broaden into fields and orchards, where

double rows of cherry trees line the long country roads, or used to. A village straggles down each brook—Wüstegiersdorf, Peterswaldau, Langenbielau—hidden one from the other by high hills. All were old mill towns. Handweaving villages in the eighteenth century, they thrived during the nineteenth after the industrial revolution.

The boundaries of Langenbielau stretch five miles along the Biele River, and, like a snake that has swallowed a frog, the village bulges to three streets wide in the middle, with its head and neck flattened at the lower end, and its tail wriggling up towards the mountains. The *Grafs* (counts) who owned the two textile mills of whitewashed brick lived on estates up in the hills, but in the village itself most of the houses were small—white or red cottages with flower gardens. The four or five houses of consequence were owned by mill officials and high personnel, the same families for generations. A *Gymnasium* (high school), a trade school, and three grammar schools were scattered through the village. There were two butcher shops, two bakers, a general store, a couple of dame stores, and even a hat shop—"*Modes*" in fancy French scroll on the window. A park toward the lower end with tanbark paths and big oaks and chestnuts ended in large farms and fields, and then the valley broadened away east-northeast to Breslau. On both sides of Langenbielau stretched vegetable gardens, orchards, and the fields.

I had visited my parents-in-law shortly after my marriage, and they had stayed with us later in Geneva, so they, and Langenbielau, were not strangers to me when we went to Silesia in the summer of 1940.

They lived in a small house with a backyard and a tiny Kate Greenaway garden that was Gerhart's father's delight. Not more than fifteen feet long and eight feet wide, it was entrancing. At the back against the fence lined with raspberry canes was a minute *Laube* (summerhouse) shaded by honeysuckles and roses, with just room enough for a table and two benches. A neat gravel path exactly in the center of the garden led to the *Laube,* bordered with alternating low gooseberry bushes and miniature standard currant trees, some bearing red berries and some white. At the entrance of the path spread two big black currant bushes in thick glossy dark foliage, their berries pungent and delicious when mixed with the others. Strawberry plants grew in neat rows behind the currant trees and gooseberries, and between them a leafy carpet of young lettuces, radishes and scallions, with tomatoes forming a back-drop. This charming little pocket garden yielded an amazing amount of fresh food and vitamins, due of course to Vater's green thumb and loving care.

Vater, my father-in-law, was a quiet, contained man, frail and small, with finely cut features. He spoke only when he had something to say. At first the children thought him severe, but when he realized that they were well-brought-up, considering their American mother, he became very fond of them. His rare smile and his strict but fair treatment soon won them over. He hated noise and disorder, and though we created both, he never lost his temper. Vater was a very intelligent man, and had he gone to a university he would undoubtedly have risen to a professorship. But he was the son of a farmer with no means for higher education.

Mutter, my mother-in-law, was a remarkable woman, and one of the best I have ever known. Pretty, even when I knew her, she was warm and lively, competent in everything she undertook and an excellent cook and housekeeper. Her natural tact and understanding soon overcame my feeling of strangeness, and we became fast friends. To my relief she had a gay and frivolous streak, always however at war with her provincial upbringing and surroundings. She had a real fear of dire poverty due to the terrible inflation period between the wars when they lost all their savings, had to sell their few valuables, and almost starved.

As a young girl, the daughter of the mill superintendent in the neighboring village of Wüstegiersdorf, Mutter had spent a year in Salzburg, which, besides broadening her horizons, had also taught her the fine points of Viennese cookery. With our meager war-time ingredients, she made every meal not only palatable and nourishing, but delicious. Also wise in country lore, she was a good nurse and cured us all with herbs, teas and poultices, common sense, patience and infinite good humor.

They were both very tolerant of their exotic and unpredictable foreign daughter-in-law. I don't think they ever quite believed the tales of my happy and irresponsible childhood in Louisville where I played the livelong day, where almost my only duty was to have my hair curled on my nurse's finger. I am sure they wrote it off as fantastic and improbable. I pulled some pretty awful blunders at first and never did give up all my wild ways. What's more, my command of German was hardly fluent. Mutter smoothed my path in that conservative, provincial little bourgeois community and was very forbearing. When her friends came to call I committed the cardinal sin of plumping myself down on the sofa, always reserved by convention for the oldest or most important guests. What was worse, I sat on one foot. But she coped with it, and I gradually learned. The townspeople, at first scandalized, soon became amused and then positively tolerant of my oddities.

I took the children out of Berlin to Langenbielau for weeks at a time during 1940 and 1941, for better food and air and for a respite from air raids.[1] While I was often bored, I was thankful to be there. I did my share in the household as best I could, awkward and slow at first, as everything was very old-fashioned. Try as I would, I never learned to make the beds *hübsch* (pretty) as Mutter was always admonishing me. I was relieved to be able to make them at all.

German bedding is monstrous, especially in the provinces. First a normal mattress, then a great thick goose-feather mattress on top of it, then the plain linen under sheet, then the upper, edged with crocheted lace, then a long hard wedge-shaped pillow, with two huge square feather ones over it, and a great hard sausage of a bolster. Over the sheet came the *Bezug* (no translation exists, for the object had no existence in the West), a thick down quilt stuffed into an over-sized, lace-edged and embroidered case, the top edge of which folded over and buttoned onto itself with crocheted buttons (as did all the pillow-cases). Covering this slippery, billowing mass was an elaborate white bedspread. And I was to make it look *hübsch*! But as it was very cold in Silesia in the winter, and no bedrooms were ever heated, I snuggled down in my feathers gratefully. I knew I couldn't be smothered, for sometime during the night the *Bezug* always slid onto the floor.

My other penance was Wash Day—a misnomer as it was Three Wash Days. It was a monthly affair, and it all began in the afternoon of the First Day.[2] We opened a large, dark

---

[1] The first British air raids in Berlin took place August 25 and 26, 1940.

[2] Given the work involved, the monthly wash is understandable. It was a mark of status to have sufficient linens to wash but once a month. On the estates of the wealthy, there were enough linens to make the wash an annual affair.

closet and dragged out bags of soiled clothes—a month's accumulation of dirty sheets, *bezug* cases, pillow-cases, bolster cases, towels, dish towels, tablecloths, napkins, and clothes—among them Vater's long heavy woolen underwear and Mutter's flannel petticoats and incredible cotton drawers with Hamburg edging, and heavy aprons. After sorting them into baskets, we lugged them to the Wash Kitchen, a small building at the end of the backyard, and made a fire in the large stove. Mutter proudly pointed out the modern conveniences: two big, set-in soapstone tubs, each with a cold water tap. We lifted a huge iron cauldron onto the stove and filled it with cold water through a hose attached to a tap—no need to carry buckets of water. While it was heated we sorted the clothes again, heavy linen and cottons, woolens, white clothes and then the *Buntstück* (colored pieces). Mutter carefully shaved a minimum of laundry soap into a tub, and we siphoned hot water into it. Then came cold water from the tap to make a nice lukewarm bath to soak the dirtiest pile overnight.

Next morning we rose at six and started the stove. We washed all day, sloshing in overshoes on the cement floor awash with soapy water. We tussled with the great sheets, scrubbing with the wash-board, and then came the great rinsing. I don't know how many cauldrons of water we heated, used, and drained off into the hole in the floor, but our backs were breaking by suppertime.

In the meantime, with Vater's help, we put up some half-dozen long poles and strung on them miles of clothesline very high. This was an intricate arrangement; it had to be just right or the lines would sag and the poles lean. A sketchy soup at noon and then back to the tubs. I had thought the worst was over, but I was mistaken. I started in quickly—almost gaily—to hang a *Bezug*. "*Nein, nein,*" shouted Mutter, "You can't do it alone!" I soon saw why. It was as heavy as sheet-iron, and there was only one way to hang it. One edge must overhang the line eight centimeters, even, all the way, and stretched out and smoothed until wrinkleless. This was more difficult than it sounds, especially if there was a wind blowing.

We washed, rinsed, wrung, and hung, and then folded the dry pieces and laid them in the proper baskets. Before folding, the sheets must be jerked. This required skill. Mutter held two ends and I the other two, and in a violent rhythmic unison she jerked her right end while I jerked my right, then left, right, left, right until she deemed they were stretched straight.

On the third day the woolens and colored pieces were washed and dried, the clothesline carefully reeled off, coiled, and put away with the poles until the next Three Wash Days. But we were not yet through. In the afternoon we went off in a picturesque procession to the *Mangel* (a large ironing press). A big basket of sheets was balanced on the little express wagon (everyone owned one in this long village, to transport groceries and baggage as well as laundry). I pulled it while Erika and Jerry pushed, and Mutter headed the procession with great dignity in her old straw hat—down the street over the rough cobbles, over the footbridge, and to the *Mangel,* one of several presses in the town. It filled a large room. Mutter stood at the head and I at the foot, and we set the great roller rolling, pressing the sheets flat and smooth. Then we filed back home. The Big Wash was over for another month.

In Langenbielau I learned to love certain German dishes that I had scorned before. Mutter was the best cook I know, and in those early days of the war we once had roast venison, wild hare several times, and a goose at Christmas, cooked with sour-sweet red-kraut and potato dumplings.

An Anglo-Saxon flour dumpling is doughy and flavorless—practically inedible to me now—but a German potato dumpling with German gravy from the roast, nicely flavored with the *Rotkraut* (red cabbage) sauce, is a different species—celestial. Made from cold boiled potatoes sliced and then diced fine, crumbled by hand and kneaded with one-third flour and an egg and salt, then rolled into a long sausage and cut deftly into oblongs on a slant, the dumplings are dropped into boiling water and removed to drain the minute they float, ready to serve.

Mutter saved her butter and sugar to bake a weekly cake while we were there: *Streusselkuchen,* as well as the rare *Möhnkuchen* (a delicious paste of sugar, milk and finely ground poppy-seed rolled into the dough as jelly in a jelly roll and my absolute favorite), and for birthdays and great occasions a *Nusskuchen* (ground nuts, usually hazel, which abounded in Silesia, made into a roll). A form of grain more or less the same taste and texture as our semolina or Cream of Wheat called *Gries* was used to thicken gravies and soups instead of flour, and I found it superior. With three stalks of asparagus and a couple of tablespoons of *Gries,* Mutter made the most delicious asparagus soup for the family.

Though I was often bored in Langenbielau, the children were carefree and happy. Before breakfast they would fetch the crisp morning breakfast rolls and the milk ration. Grossvater made the fire in the big porcelain stove with briquettes that lasted until evening, gave a great deal of heat, and were extremely economical, with no dirt. There were warm seats on the stove and a big warmer for the food. Before breakfast, Mutter and I aired the bedding, and after the dishes were done made the beds and were ready for the dusting, cleaning, marketing, and preparing dinner.

There were many children in the neighborhood. A little boy Jerry's age, Dieter Märtens, came to stay with his grandmother three houses away, and there were Rosel and Gisel Richter next door, two charming little sisters, both older than Erika, who took charge of all the games and dealt impartially with the children, boys and girls, older and younger. They both looked like children in fairy tales—rosy, with blond pigtails and high cheekbones.

Sunday was a very special day, particularly in summer. I thought of it thankfully as The Day the Bedding Wasn't Aired. After church there was an early dinner and a short rest for the old people. Then Grossmutter packed slices of cake in a napkin in a little basket, and we all five started off for the afternoon—Erika skipping ahead, Vater and I walking sedately after, and Mutter and Gertli (as she called Jerry) bringing up the rear. Jerry's short legs and Grossmutter's rheumatic ones were gaited to the same pace.

There were two choices in summer: Steinhauser and the Goldenes Sieb. The latter was our favorite, though it involved a longer walk, at least three miles up the ever-climbing street, until it became a country lane, always following the river Biele. We gradually climbed to the forest and the mountains. There in a sun-dappled clearing was the Golden Sieve, a rustic coffee house with tables and benches under great oaks. We ordered a big, china pot of ersatz coffee, usually called *malz* coffee because it had some malt in it, and Mutter spread out the cake on a big napkin. The children played in the brook and the trout pool, and I walked a little way into the forest. Then we had the long walk back again, weary when we reached home, but full of sun and air and well-being. Sunday supper differed from weekdays in two respects. Instead of potato salad, we had the cold, leftover dumplings, fried like potatoes, and a glass of real tea instead of linden or some other herb tea. Some of Mutter's tisanes were very good. We picked fresh, tender, young wild strawberry and blackberry leaves, for instance, and they made a delicious infusion. Many other herbs made teas for coughs, fevers, rheumatism, or worms.

On other summer Sundays we walked across the upland fields and along a cherry-bordered road to the nearest mountain and an inn called Steinhauser, which lay snuggled against it. The great forest started abruptly behind the Inn and stretched dark and romantic above and to all sides of us, an enchanted forest like that in a Grimm's fairy tale, with no underbrush.

In 1941 the children and I took a room for most of the summer and on through Christmas at Steinhauser Inn. We came upon fairy circles of toadstools and, pushing up through the dark floor of soft pine needles, the brilliant *Fligenpilz* (a mushroom), with its scarlet and orange spots, beloved of elves, but deadly poisonous to the unenchanted. We often saw roe-buck, and sometimes the rarer *Muflon* (mountain sheep). But we liked best the lower, more open woods of beech and birch where the light came through and the birds sang. In the clearings in the late afternoon, hares played Ring-Around-a-Rosie. Here we picnicked and played, waded and dabbled in the clear trout streams, and Erika and Jerry grew brown and healthy. We picked wild strawberries and raspberries and were allowed to eat all the fallen plums in the inn's orchard—purple pear-shaped plums and the sweet little green *Mirabellen*, thus storing up vitamins against the winter to come. All through the fall in the rutting season, we heard the stags bugling through the forest and the mountains echoing back.

That February, while we were back staying with the grandparents, Erika started school in Langenbielau. This was a very important day, and her grandfather managed to find an old *Tornister*, the satchel without which no self-respecting German child could possibly start school. An almost square leather bag with the hair of the cow on the outside, it had straps that went over the shoulders like a rucksack. Around her neck on a strap so long it flapped against her stomach hung a smaller leather lunch box. This left both Erika's arms free for rope skipping, ball or snowball throwing, and for defense against any sudden attack.

She started out scrubbed and rosy, pigtails neat and shiny, slate pencil sharpened and her sponge, properly moistened but not too wet, dangling outside on a short string so as not to wet the contents of the bag. (I never saw a child in Germany with his sponge inside!) In the lunch box reposed two neatly wrapped sandwiches of dark bread, one with margarine and the other with *Wurst*. Ordinarily, an apple or another fruit completed the lunch. But on this first day she proudly carried a large paper *tüte*, a cornucopia filled with a few hard candies and a peppermint stick to avert homesickness and tears. It was a good school, and Erika loved it.

It was in Langenbielau that Erika went to the "*Kinderschar*," a kind of Nazi Cub Scout club. It was the only organization she ever took part in and was mostly nature training for the little kids. Of course, they had to salute the swastika and say "Heil Hitler," but there was nothing I could do about it. We had managed to avoid it in Berlin.

Chapter Two

BERLIN
1942 to August 1943
Voices of Doom

THE JAPANESE BOMBED Pearl Harbor on December 7, 1941; four days later, Germany declared war on the United States. By 1942 the entire world seemed to be in a conflagration, with war on three continents.

Gerhart's job at the Deutsches Institut für Aussenpolitische Forschung involved research and the publication of various booklets and articles, mostly propaganda for the Reich. He also served as a minor advisor to the Foreign Office. In this position, he sided with the faction that adamantly opposed Germany's war against Russia. Opposition to Germany's foreign policy led Gerhart to end his connection with the Institut and the Foreign Office in the beginning of 1943. He accepted the chair in American history and civilization at Berlin University's Department of International Affairs.

Gerhart never did take up his teaching duties. Instead, he was assigned the task of evacuating the Department's half million volumes, which he called "the most valuable library on international affairs on this continent." They were moved to a fourteenth-century church in Beeskow, halfway between Berlin and Frankfort, and by the time the job was complete, he later wrote, the church was "like a gigantic Faustus' study." Gerhart copied the entire card catalogue, keeping one set in

Beeskow and the other in Berlin, and instituted a daily courier service. Gerhart's "Faustus' study" was the only public library in Germany that continued to function all through the war.

Meanwhile, Mary and the children moved back and forth between the city and the country, despite the fact that after Hitler's decision to aim the Blitzkrieg at London in September 1940, the Allies' bombing raids on Berlin occurred with increasing frequency.

We had spent all of the winter of 1941 in Berlin, and we returned for part of the winter of 1942. When we had first arrived from Geneva, I had been shocked to see that on the paths of our neighborhood park in Innsbrucker Platz among the green benches there were a number painted yellow, which had been set aside for the Jews. If the yellow ones were all full on warm summer afternoons, I and most of the other sitters naturally made room for the Jews on our benches. All the children, Jew and Gentile alike, played together in the sand-pile and jumped from the pergola. Then during 1941 the Jews began to disappear completely. At first some were allowed to leave the country, though their possessions were confiscated. Gradually those remaining were taken off at night, a few at a time. One morning they were there, the next they had vanished. We knew they had been taken to concentration camps, but we didn't know then what happened there. It wasn't just Jews who vanished; many non-Jewish Germans were also being spirited away, guilty of holding unacceptable political views or protesting the actions of the Reich, guilty of being homosexual, guilty of any one of numerous things that were unacceptable to Hitler and his government. Their families would hear nothing of their arrests or their whereabouts or their crimes for weeks and months, sometimes only after a man or woman had been condemned or executed. We knew many had been killed, but not until after the War did I know of the systematic extermination nor of the infamous methods used. It was all so secret. Unless one lived near one of the camps, few even knew where they were.

The British air raids sent us down to the cellar almost every night: out the front door onto the street, duck into a narrow back passage and then dash over a black inner courtyard and down some steps into the cellar of the next apartment house, a large, crowded room lit by one or two candles. Often there would be only an interval of five to ten minutes between the *Voralarm* (warning) and the real *Fliegeralarm*, followed immediately by the bombs. Several times we were caught in the passage, or worse, in the courtyard, with falling flak and debris. The bombing became so continuous and set off so many fires that we women went in shifts all during the night up dark, steep steps through the vast attics and onto the roof to put the fires out with sand and shovels. (There were no men with us—they had to go to factories, hospitals and government buildings to fight fires—and the teen-aged boys were all in the *Flak* [anti-aircraft]). Some of our acquaintances had sons of fourteen or fifteen, and it was an anxious time for the parents.

There were, of course, many casualties. Every night was cold and most were windy. The whole sky was aglow with fire, and a constant rain of cinders and burning bits of debris fell on us. Since we went up in shifts, there were always a few women left with the gang of children. The littlest ones all slept through the night on some mattresses, but Erika and the older ones were often awake and lonely, and she usually stayed near Jerry. I hated leaving them alone, but there was nothing else to do.

The British had begun to practice what they called "area bombing," using *drück* or pressure bombs (high explosive bombs that blew out windows and roofs and exposed the interior of buildings to incendiary bombs). These were like nothing we had yet experienced. A whole block would be struck at once, bursting in a holocaust of flames that spread quickly for miles. Next morning under the smoke, nothing was left but a wilderness of smoldering debris. The odd thing was that always one or two houses would be completely untouched—or with just one wall stripped off to show an almost neat interior like a doll's house, bathrooms with blackened towels folded on the rack, carpeted staircases, a child's room with toys on a shelf. Another strange thing: a person standing in a doorway half a mile away would be found flattened against the wall, killed by the pressure.

I found the *Voralarm* the most nerve-shattering part of the bombing cycle. It came out of the blue, when one was unprepared. I can conceive of no more terrifying sound than that inhuman wail, rising and falling and rising again, vibrating simultaneously over the big city, penetrating every corner with a shattering insistence. If there were a Voice of Doom foretelling the end of the world, that would be it.

When the real alarm came—at first about twenty minutes after the warning, and, as the raids increased in size and frequency, ten to five minutes later—one was prepared. We were either in the shelter or on our way. The all-clear signal at first meant blessed relief; it meant that the bombers had stopped short of Berlin or taken another route. Later, it was only a brief respite before another warning, although the all-clear siren was given after every attack. From 1943 on we often had scarcely left the shelter before another *Vor-*

alarm sent us back. It is hard to imagine now the constant tension everyone lived in while performing daily duties. Taking risks became normal.

In February of 1943 scarlet fever swept over Berlin, and Erika got it. Like most European apartment houses, ours had little shops on the ground floor. Unfortunately one of these sold butter and milk, and no one with a contagious disease was permitted to stay in a building where food was sold. All the hospitals were hopelessly overcrowded and inadequately staffed, so the children's physician had to send Erika to a makeshift scarlet fever ward. She had a raging fever, so they sent her in an ambulance. I followed, getting there a few hours later. The ward was a drafty gym in a school, and the door was opened by a little patient! The children lay in a long line of cots, the very ill and the convalescent together in the great bare gym, with the wind blowing in each time the door was opened.

Two days later Jerry broke out, and our pediatrician, with great perseverance, managed to get both Jerry and Erika into a children's hospital north of the city. It took me two hours to get there by subway and tram, as so many of the lines had been hit. They were there six weeks and the worst of it was that the hospital was in an industrial area, so it was a constant target. It had already been bombed twice and rebuilt. I never knew until I reached the hospital whether the children had survived the night's raids. It was now almost useless to try to get private telephone calls through.

The children had definite air-raid instructions. At the warning alarm they were to put on their slippers. Erika was at once to go quickly down the corridor and stairs into the cellar. Jerry had equally strict orders to wait for a nurse to take him. One night (I found this out later) the warning came, and Erika obeyed as usual. Very shortly bombs began to fall in the neighborhood and she suddenly realized Jerry wasn't there. A substitute nurse's aide had forgotten him. The raid was over by the time he was finally down. He said afterwards that when he heard the bombs he had decided to come by himself, but he couldn't find his slippers in the dark and so didn't dare. But he said he was not very frightened. (Most children weren't frightened during raids, if there were other children there and at least one calm adult.)

Life in Berlin was quite disrupted now. Much as I hated the ugly city, I admired the Berliners. They were a tough bunch with plenty of stamina. I was amazed to find how openly they grumbled about the government and stuck out their necks—both men and women during the early war years. The average housewife standing in line for queues day after day didn't hesitate to say openly what she thought of the whole damn system. There were quite violent arguments on the street, pro- and anti-Nazi. But they all wanted to win the war and were, of course, bitter against the British and American bombs. I spoke English with the children openly in Berlin and had only two unpleasant reactions. Berlin was, after all, a big cosmopolitan city, so ugly in itself, though the parks and green squares in the heart of the city were beautiful, and the outer suburbs were attractive, set in lovely sandy forests with many lakes.

Erika never went back to school. By the time she was well, all the grade schools had ceased to function. More than half of the school buildings in the city had been destroyed. Many entire blocks in our neighborhood were now reduced to rubble. One immense fire when Wittenburg Platz was razed ignited our roof many times during the night and the next twenty-four hours. This was an inferno. There seemed always to be a wind, which spread the fire for miles. Some subways were still running, but now it was almost impossible to pick one's way downtown among the debris.

By the summer of 1943 there was American day bombing on a big scale. From then on I dreaded being far away from the children, shopping only for needed supplies, hearing the warning and running to get home before the actual bombs fell. We no longer felt safe in the cellar. There were too many cases of the great concrete, brick, and stone buildings collapsing and burying those inside, or of water pipes struck and everyone drowned.

Joseph Goebbels, the minister of propaganda, had issued an edict that all women with small children, and all children, must leave Berlin by the first of August or be evacuated by the government. In June 1943, I packed up the children, my silver, best linen, and some books and went to Langenbielau, intending to stay with Mutter until we found a room, but there was no room to be had in the town or in any neighboring village. Neaby Breslau was also impossible. Relatives from Berlin had already swamped the whole province of Silesia. The grandparents had barely enough fuel for the one stove, but we stayed with them until the approach of the forced migration made me desperate. An American friend who had also married a German had promised to write to her sister-in-law, the wife of a pastor in Stargard-in-Pommern, on my behalf. We were fortunate; the sister-in-law had found us room and board with a pastor's family in a Pomeranian village not too far from Stargard.

In 1943 the northeastern provinces were the quietest and least troubled part of Germany. Russian bombing raids had so far been negligible. I was also pleased because, except for Berlin, I had lived only in the east of Germany, where few tourists find their way. It is the part I knew and liked the best. Though Bavaria is beautiful with its Alpine scenery, I didn't like the Bavarians I had met. I had a dim view of Rhinelanders, sometimes derided as *falsch* (phony) by Northerners; nor did I especially relate to the Saxons. But with the north Germans, I felt at home: East Prussians, Pomeranians, Brandenburgers from the Mark, Mecklenburgers, Holsteiners, all Prussians except the last-named.

The word "Prussian," anathema to Americans after the First World War, had a different connotation for me. It meant country people, both farmers and landed gentry. I found them very much like the English and the old-fashioned New Englander, both in tradition and mentality. They were perhaps lacking in imagination, sometimes conservative and stolid, but I still liked them. They had good solid qualities: honesty, integrity, dignity, and a love of the land, and usually a sense of humor.

After a brief trip to Berlin, I arrived at the train station to return to Breslau and collect Erika. I found a scene of mob panic. Everyone was trying to get out of Berlin before the mass evacuation. Hitherto calm, reasonable women were battling to push their children onto trains. A man already on the train finally pulled me through a broken window. After this experience I decided the quicker I got to Pomerania, the better. Frau Pastor Schwarz might take in someone else to avoid being flooded with Goebbels's evacuees. I decided to leave Jerry with his grandparents temporarily and head straight for Pomerania, and so in Breslau Erika and I boarded a train going north toward Stettin. It was the last comfortable train ride I had in Germany.

Ten days later, our Berlin apartment house was bombed and the whole *Platz* (square) destroyed.

Chapter Three

POMERANIA
August 1943 to 1944
The Big Sky

IN 1943 ALLIED BOMBING intensified with widespread damage throughout Germany: in Berlin, Stuttgart, Stettin, Düsseldorf, Cologne, Hamburg, and Nuremberg.

Looking for a safe haven, Mary and the children arrived in Barnimskunow in the August heat. For centuries, Pomerania and Mecklenburg had been the chief agricultural lands of Germany. Life there was quite unlike anything Mary had ever experienced. For the next year and a half, Mary, Erika, and Jerry would be paying guests in two village homes. Despite the scarcity of food and clothing—and the existence of a prisoner-of-war camp on the outskirts of town—the war seemed far away from this sleepy, conservative village.

News of what was happening elsewhere in Germany came from secretly listening to BBC broadcasts and through letters from Gerhart, who continued working on the library in Beeskow.

Pommern, pronounced *Pummern*, stretches from west to east along the Baltic Sea in a long and beautiful coastline of pine forests, dunes, and picturesque islands. Vor-Pommern, about one-fifth of the province, is a rough wedge from the Oder River between the sea and Mecklenburg, dwindling to a point just beyond Stralsund and including the Island of Rugen. Most of the province is poor, sandy soil, but German patience and industry long ago redeemed much of the arid land until it rivaled Mecklenburg in farm production. Together they were the breadbasket of Germany. I happened to land in an area lying south and east of Stettin known as the Puritzer *Weizen-Aker* (Puritz Wheat Acres). Until the First World War, it had always been sown in wheat, though later it was transformed into sugar-beet fields.

Erika and I changed trains at Stettin and then at Stargard, twenty-five miles southeast, for the local branch. We were dropped off at a tiny station that stood empty in the midst of fields, while the little train puffed its way south to the small town of Pyritz. Not a house was in sight, only a wide, flat land stretching endlessly under a vast sky. The only sound was the clip-clop of a horse and buggy disappearing rapidly on the road going west. We turned east along the same road, which ran straight and cobbled, high above the fields. It was narrow, like a Roman road, and a double row of ancient elms provided a grateful shade. The treetops met at the far horizon, where a sharp bend in the road concealed everything except a church spire thrusting through the large clump of deep, summer green.

I knew Barnimskunow was east of the railroad, but that was all I knew. Other distant lines of trees indicated other roads. Coming from the mountains and forests, Pomerania seemed strangely empty. Erika exclaimed over the flatness, and we were already homesick. But during the two years we were there, we gradually discovered its charm—the big sky, like the sky over our American West.

We picked up our light suitcases and started along the road in the haze of the August heat. As we came to the sharp bend in the road, the fields yielded to green pastures with a few horses grazing inside white fences, almost like Kentucky. Then we noticed a pretty village on our left, but the road by-passed it. Erika looked white and tired, and I was hopeful when a horse and cart drove out from the village and the pretty girl driving stopped. "Is this Barnimskunow?" I asked.

"Oh no, this is Warnitz. Barnimskunow is two kilometers further. Get in, I'll be glad to take you. I live there."

Her name was Hanni, and she was the baker's daughter, about to return home after delivering bread to Warnitz. Soon the road merged into a long, long street with small brick cottages set back in tiny gardens. We were in Barnimskunow. We told Hanni we were going to the parsonage. "Oh, to Frau Schwarz's." I thought she raised her eyebrows. So far we had seen no human; only, to our astonishment, hundreds of geese feeding noisily in a big pond where the road widened. The long street at last made a sharp right angle, and a big manor house appeared, set back in a leafy park with iron fence and gate. Just beyond the turn, there was an old, rosy brick church set inside a churchyard walled in with the same mellow brick. Hanni set us down at the *Pfarrhaus* (Parsonage), a square house within the churchyard wall and a little apple orchard behind it.

Frau Schwarz met us at the door of the *Pfarrhaus* with a warm welcome, though she had not yet received my letter. After a cup of real coffee, we were installed in what had been her dining room, pleasant and airy and not too crowded even with the three comfortable cots.

Frau Schwarz was eager to have us as paying guests, otherwise "Goebbels would dump God knows who" on her. She already had the family of a steel worker from the Ruhr, a woman and three children, "and Catholic at that."

The Pastor was in Greece, a chaplain with the Army, but the Pastor's wife was a most amazing woman. I have never seen her like before or since. Broad-shouldered and muscular, she possessed such an excess of physical and nervous energy that only in the pioneer days of the American West could she have fulfilled her destiny. In this sleepy, conservative village she could find no vent for her surplus energy except in mischief. She was excellent company, for she was extremely intelligent and quite witty. She was shrewd and drove a hard bargain and swapped like a horse trader. Her straight dark hair was strained back into a hard knot, and behind thick glasses her dark eyes, large and slightly protuberant, were intense and penetrating. At first I found her almost physically repellant, but her sudden brilliant smile transfigured her. Though she was plain, she apparently had great physical charm for some men; it was obvious she was passionate, both temperamentally and physically.

Frau Schwarz had a melodramatic streak that caused her to exaggerate the most trivial things. She kept the village in an uproar. She feuded with everyone, particularly her patron, Herr Michels (Mickels), owner of the estate, and Herr Schultz, the village schoolmaster, and his family. But she kept the parish books faithfully and competently, kept the Church clean and decent, dined the visiting pastor who came monthly to conduct services and laundered his surplice, though she had no use for him. She did all the church chores when the old sexton died and was ready to dig a grave if need be. Her passions were black coffee, cigarettes, motorbikes, thrillers, and first and foremost, her husband and children. As she was now almost entirely deprived of the first five items, she concentrated on the last.

As soon as Erika and I were settled in, I left her to the mercy of the Schwarz clan to go back to Silesia and pick up Jerry. He was loath to leave Gross-mutter and his friend Dieter Märtens, and besides, the strawberries in Gross-vater's garden were ripening. I stayed in Langenbielau one night and then we had to say *Auf Wiedersehen* until we met again. Alas, it turned out to be farewell, for it was the last time we ever saw Vater and Mutter.

Once Jerry and I were back in Barnimskunow and the big oak door of the *Pfarrhaus* closed on us, we were embroiled in domestic bedlam: noise, confusion, and drama. This was to be our home for an indefinite period!

The Schwarz children were all individuals. Ernst-Wilhelm, the eldest at twelve, was short and muscular for his age, with a small delicate nose, hard eyes and a cruel mouth. He was intelligent like his mother, and like her, very nervous and high-strung. When he was happy having his own way and in high spirits, he was rather attractive. Christian, who was about ten, tall and awkward, was non-competitive, non-combative, and rather dreamy, but his most engaging quality was his sweet-tempered sunny disposition. He was two years older than Erika and her favorite playmate. Next, but certainly not least, was Puppe. (Her mouthful of a name was Ilse-Maria but she was known as *Puppe* (doll) in the family and Puppe-Pastor throughout the village.) She was a fascinating elfin child, but one to be reckoned with, as we later found out. Slender and graceful, with fine, wispy brown hair, and a pale clear skin, her large green eyes were quick and intelligent and saw everything. Her sense of drama—and of the ridiculous—was highly developed, and she could be quite irresistible at times. She was an imaginative liar, however, and I think believed in her own lies.

The fourth Schwarz was a character and a darling. Jürgen was just Jerry's age, not yet five, and they became boon companions. Stocky and sturdy with dark, shiny, straight hair, rosy cheeks and great solemn brown eyes, he was the only silent Schwarz. He never spoke. His independence, self-sufficiency, and perseverance were amazing. He paid no attention to anyone but Jerry, except when the Schwarz clan ganged up. He had a pair of high black boots he wore constantly, but when he had to take them off, the process took him twenty minutes and sometimes half an hour. Yet he never asked anyone to help him, and no one ever did. He'd tug and tug and get redder and redder, but never a word. He and Jerry roamed the village and fields for scraps of old iron, tin, wire, string, and leather until they had a high mound in the *Pfarrhaus Hof* (the big, square cobbled yard). There they'd sit for hours sorting them out and "selling" them, with scarcely a word.

The last and fifth Schwarz was a cunning, bright, little blond girl of eighteen months named Crista, but called by the family and the village *Schwesterchen* (little sister). Our *Hof* had once been covered with cobbles, but the Schwarzes had pulled the stones out gradually so that the surface was very uneven and muddy. Crista's delight was to be careened wildly back and forth in a rickety old baby carriage by her devoted brothers and sister. One would push her at a run and let her bounce to another, who then shoved her violently back. She often fell out but never cried. She was most like her brother Christian.

There were two helpers with Frau Schwarz when I first went there. Herta, a young woman from the village, was Frau Pastor's assistant and made the wheels go round. Herta was brisk and efficient, always cheerful and smiling, but didn't hesitate to lash out with her tongue or a hand to an impudent or disobedient child. Anna, from an orphanage, was a big, strong, blond Polish girl with German nationality. She was lazy and phlegmatic and got out of all the work she could, but helped with the enormous wash, fed Frau Schwarz's two pigs when the boys neglected them, and was generally good-humored. It was a jolly household most of the time, though incredibly noisy, everyone outshouting the others to be heard. Nothing was taken up or put down without a clatter, and all inanimate objects seemed to lead a lively life of their own. But soon I saw there really was order in the chaos, and the order was Herta.

In all the Pomeranian houses the kitchen, pantries, and corridor floors were of polished red brick, slippery and very cold in winter. Before we took it over, the family had gathered in the large dining room, but now we ate in the nursery where the four younger children slept. The furniture in this nursery/dining room consisted of cots, battered wardrobes, and chests of drawers lined up around the walls, with two big wood plank tables in the center. Everything was wobbly, scratched and gouged, with most of the paint peeled off. At any time of the day or night there might be a child on top of a wardrobe, ready to hurl a ball or a pillow at a passer-by. Door and drawer handles had long since been yanked off.

There were only three chairs in the room. Since, with the Ruhr family who lived in a large attic room, there were thirteen of us, the announcement of each meal was accompanied by a great clattering. In came an assortment of ten chairs on the run, atop the heads of the larger children and pushed along the floor by the little ones. Meals were on the dot and any child more than one minute late got no dinner, which seemed reasonable given the chaotic situation.

Herta and I brought in the food and we all stood until the last child was in place, then Frau Pastor named a child to say grace. The instant "Amen" was uttered, down we sat and the meal began. At the table at least, Frau Schwarz insisted on manners. Each child could talk in turn on signal from the head of the table. Giggling or whispering or whining or not emptying your plate meant instant banishment with no more food. Choking or sneezing or belching brought only a severe reprimand if a first offense. With that lively crew to whom self-expression in any form was the breath of life, there was a vacant seat at every meal. After we'd finished, the children took the chairs out and then the dishes. Sometimes there was a magnificent crash, but surprisingly few dishes were broken.

Once we had fish for dinner, which I had brought home from Stargard. Frau Schwarz announced that everyone would eat all his fish bones! There would be no waste of precious minerals. I thought she was joking, but every child began munching fish bones. No Schwarz child ever disobeyed his mother's public edicts. I protested that I would not eat them nor did my children have to. But they did and survived. Fortunately, we couldn't get fish often.

It was strictly against the law for anyone to make butter. All the milk from every farm must be taken to the nearest dairy, where the butter production and distribution were supervised. The farmers had to buy their butter and cheese on their ration cards, receiving less than they were accustomed to, but more than non-producers. This law held for all farm products. Pigs, sheep, goats, and fowl were regulated according to the number of mouths on the farm. If a family were entitled to one pig, for instance, it could only be slaughtered at a certain age and weight, and its owner could keep only part of it.

Frau Pastor obeyed few laws, even if the penalty was imprisonment. She never got caught, though most people knew she had more than she was entitled to. She kept two pigs and two goats from whose milk she made butter regularly. Sugar being very scarce, we had few desserts. But twice when Herr Pastor sent a package of raisins from Greece, we had a feast. Herta beat a great bowl of cottage cheese until it was light and fluffy, added a little milk and a very little sugar, and stirred in the raisins. Delicious!

That first Christmas in Pommern in 1943 Herr Pastor came home briefly on leave. There was wild rejoicing. I was very curious to see him. He was broad and solid and handsome, I thought, dark and ruddy like Jürgen, and quiet, too, like him. But he was pathologically bad-tempered. His children were not in awe of him, for no one really daunted them except their mother, but they were subdued when he was present. His wife radiated joy like a sunflower turning to the sun. Incredible though it seemed to me, they were lovers on the grand scale. She was very frank about it, glowed and sparkled and looked almost beautiful

I had continually ignored Puppe's fantastic lies as they hadn't affected us, but at Christmas there was an absurd though most unpleasant incident. She informed the household that Erika and Jerry had stolen a large, heart-shaped Christmas cookie intended for their father from the traditional cookie platter. My children denied this hotly. They never lied, and I had no reason to believe they were lying now. Frau Schwarz, dramatic as always, treated it as a major crime. I stoutly stood up for them and told her that of course they hadn't taken it, but had they done so, it was no crime, and for a grown woman to make such a fuss about a cookie was ridiculous.

My attitude was even worse than the children's crime! I was ungrateful! I lacked principles! A day later two oranges Herr Schwarz had brought from Greece were missing—again the Jentschs. Herta saved the day by finding both the oranges and the half-eaten heart cookie in a corner of the study. She said she knew positively that Erika and Jerry had never been in that room. We all lost our tempers and, ridiculous as it was, relations were strained all during the holidays. I think Frau Schwarz believed Puppe, though she had often said she was a liar. Puppe was the terror of the village with her lies and pranks, yet when they talked of Puppe-Pastor it was always with a mixture of disapproval and admiration and sometimes even affection, for she was very sensitive and warm-hearted and took any village tragedy very hard.

* * * * * *

We were so absorbed in the Pastor's household that it took me some time to know the rest of Barnimskunow. I found the whole village set-up very interesting and entertaining. North German country life—in Pomerania, West and East Prussia, Mecklenburg and the Mark (E. Brandenburg)—differed sharply from the rest of Germany. For centuries these were the most important farming provinces, especially Pomerania and Mecklenburg, while the great evergreen forests of East Prussia furnished much of Germany's timber and livestock. (Pommern was particularly famous for its geese and a handsome breed of farm horse.)

The houses, barns, and *Hofs* were old and solid and picturesque, but most of the land was owned by the aristocracy and country gentry as in England. The social hierarchy was based upon rank rather than professions or education. It seemed feudal and outrageous to my American eyes. The landowner or *Gutbesitzer* lived near the village, usually at one end, in a handsome seventeenth- or eighteenth-century manor house surrounded by a large park. Sometimes there was an artificial lake and formal garden. The landowner owned his laborers' cottages in the village or rented to them in perpetuity. He was also the patron of the Established Church, the *Evangelische Kirche*. The only fly in his very rich ointment was the village school, which was run by the state and over which he had no jurisdiction.

The *Gutbesitzer* hired an *Inspektor* (like an English Superintendent) to run his estate, but even in peacetime he did a great deal himself. The *Inspektor*—an educated man, especially trained for the purpose—lived with his family in a good house with orchards, poultry, and vegetable and flower gardens, all of which belonged to his employer but which he could use as his own. After the *Gutbesitzer* in rank came the *Pastor*, the *Inspektor*, and officially the schoolmaster, but he was not always accepted by the gentry. The schoolmaster was often a thorn in the landowner's flesh—either a local radical or a city man, one as bad as the other. In truth, the schoolmaster often had little in common with the others. He was usually better educated than they, for they were a horsey lot like the English, interested mostly in each other and the country.

On the next rung in the social scale, came the *Bauern* or independent farmers, followed by the innkeepers, the millers, the general store owners, and somewhat lower, the butcher and the baker. Last were the farm laborers—the cottagers—the largest class.

Of course the system was flexible enough to allow for outstanding personalities. If the individual *Inspektor, Pastor,* or schoolmaster (or his wife) was unusually congenial or attractive, he was accepted freely by the gentry; if the contrary, he was asked to dinner or *Kaffeetrinken* twice a year and otherwise left to himself.

Barnimskunow followed this pattern. The landowner, Herr Michels, was not of the nobility and his manor house was not as handsome nor his park as extensive as some, but his field acreage was immense. His grandfather had come north from Saxony and bought large tracts of land from two local counts. He took the larger house for himself and put his *Inspektor* in the more modest one. The Michels family had always been considered outsiders, and the present incumbent was not beloved by any of the social classes. He and his wife were old and often not in residence. The older son, Rickard, known as a playboy, was now in the Army.

The *Inspektor,* Oskar Hecker, was a native Pomeranian but, though honest and hard-working, not particularly intelligent. He toadied to Herr Michels and, according to the village gossip, bullied the laborers. Ilse Hecker was no asset. Also born and bred in Pomerania, from the northeastern city of Stolp, she was a large, humorless woman, very much impressed with her own importance. She had made her *Abitur* (equivalent to a B.A.) and was very conscious of her superiority. No one had much respect for her, least of all Frau Schwarz. They had had a feud long ago and the Schwarz children continually fanned the flames, especially the seven-year-old Puppe Pastor.

Next to the Parsonage was a large independent farm owned by an elderly couple named Durre, pronounced "Durrer," with all the Pomeranian virtues. They also owned the local inn and tavern, as well as the general store. These were all housed in a big building facing the street. Their farmhouse was behind it, and their orchards, gardens, and fields beyond that. The only son was more or less of an invalid, but there were two capable daughters, Fraulein Lise and Frau Else Wegener. Both had a good head for business and had been well educated in private boarding schools. Here their likeness ended. Fraulein Lise was always pleasant enough to me and quite pretty, but rather sharp and shrewish with her sister, of whom she was jealous.

Else Wegener, the younger sister, was an outstanding person. She made life bearable and pleasant for me and became one of my closest friends. She had all the solid qualities of a north German country woman. But she was much more. Extremely tolerant of all human frailty, she had great tact. She got along with everyone in the village, cottagers and gentry alike, knew their characters and family history inside out and all the children's names and ages. She was the only person who mingled freely with all classes. Everyone told her their troubles and went to her for advice. Her outstanding characteristics, besides her innate kindness and friendly warmth, were common sense and wisdom of the country variety. Her mainspring was her interest in people. She was not above a good gossip and was often gay and amusing. She sometimes roundly berated a wayward village girl for dallying with a soldier, or scolded a lax or lazy mother. But her warmth, a great tolerance, and her interest took out the sting. She radiated that good German quality of comfort and sociability, *Gemütlichkeit*.

After her schooling, Else had traveled in Germany and once to Italy with various well-to-do school friends, who had remained devoted to her. She married an *Inspektor*, and they had lived for ten happy years on a distant estate. Then he died, leaving her a young widow with three little children. She came home, and her father built her a substantial house on his property with a garden adjoining the Rectory.

When the war came, Else and Lise were forced by the Nazi government to run the store alone, as no help could be got, and it was the only store to supply three villages. It was a terrific job in wartime, and they spent most of their time at it. Mountains of ration coupons from customers had to be tallied with the store stubs, sorted into innumerable categories, and pasted laboriously into different books. Accounting to the Government for each coupon was a grim chore, and a storekeeper had to be on the alert with every gram that was purchased. Later, I used to help with the sorting and pasting—a monthly duty that sometimes took all day Sunday and a couple of nights until midnight—in the great hall of the Durre tavern.

During the war the inn wasn't open and only occasionally was there any beer to sell in the tavern. Else's older son, Karl, was in the army, and her daughter, Eva, quite a beauty, returned to help in the store after boarding school and the stint of farm or other labor that was required of all teenagers by the government. Ernst, twelve, worked on the farm when he was not in school. The old Durres died, one soon after the other, the first year I was there, and the sisters had to carry on as best they could, with the help of an old Polish man who had always worked for them, and another Pole from the P.O.W. barracks.

It took me quite a while to learn all the workings of the village, but as my German improved, the pieces gradually fit into place.

The schoolhouse was directly across the street from

us, and the schoolmaster, Herr Schultz, an irascible, elderly man, had a house adjoining. He was an old-fashioned teacher and very strict, rapping the children's fingers frequently. The lower grades were taught by a pleasant, intelligent, young woman whom all the children loved.

Lehrer Schultz was the only Party member in the village as far as I knew, and people were cautious in his presence, all but Frau Pastor. There was a standing feud between them. A hen of his was killed on the street—run over according to the Parsonage—and we had it for dinner. Everyone was sure Ernst-Wilhelm had killed it, but it was never proved. Frau Schwarz was very anti-Nazi, as were many of the others there.[3]

Else Wegener told me that earlier Herr Pastor had preached a couple of outspoken anti-Hitler sermons at his wife's instigation. She was always sticking her neck out but was so shrewd that she was never actually caught. It was mainly, I think, that in spite of her temper, her mannish ways, and her hard bargaining, the cottagers and the townspeople all secretly liked and even admired her. She could speak their language and be very jovial and democratic.

There was a *Hitler Jugend* (Hitler Youth) and a *Bund Deutscher Mädchen* (League of German Girls) that met irregularly in another village. Herr Schultz saw to it that many of the cottagers' children went when they felt like it, but ours didn't, and we were always able to elude Herr Schultz. I think he was afraid of Frau Schwarz.

About a week after we arrived in Barnimskunow, Goebbel's influx of women and children was in full swing. We got no Berliners, but a whole large suburb from the Ruhr

---

[3] As late as 1945, only ten percent of the German population were members of the Nazi party.

swelled our population until it was bursting at the seams. They were quartered in attics, outbuildings, and cottage parlors—in every possible and impossible corner. As all these families were Catholic, a priest was brought and they used "our" church. Erika's grade was doing geography, studying the Oder River, its surroundings, and its great delta. The Ruhrites protested that they didn't want to know about the Oder—what was it to them?—so a teacher was imported and they had their own class where they could learn about Castrop-Rauxall and the Ruhrgebiet!

That fall, early, we had a pleasant diversion in the visit of Frau Schwarz's parents and her youngest sister, Crista. To my great surprise, not only Crista but her elderly parents were charming. Quiet, tactful and agreeable, they couldn't have been more of a contrast to Frau Pastor outwardly, though they all were intelligent with strong personalities. Herr Wellmann, Frau Schwarz's father, was a pastor (as was his father before him and his wife's father) in a town in Vor-Pommern. There was strong family solidarity among the whole big clan and great devotion. Frau Schwarz had four sisters and five brothers! The Schwarz children swarmed over their grandparents and their gay young aunt. I gradually heard about the other aunts and uncles, one of whom lived with her husband and children in Mexico.

When the apples in our orchard were ripe, we had a great picking. The older children swarmed in the trees, and Frau Schwarz was in her element. There were about eight different varieties of apples—the delicious, old-fashioned apples of my childhood and many new to me. They were all sorted carefully for species and size and laid out on the floor of a handsome, paneled room that must have formerly been used for parish affairs. Every apple was put down separately, and every few days we turned them over. They lasted all winter and added a great deal to our diet.

The walnuts on the other side of the churchyard wall on Herr Michels' property ripened, and Ernst-Wilhelm and Christian and Erika climbed into the trees from the wall and picked them with Frau Schwarz's tacit consent. I let this pass, but when Frau Schwarz actually sent them out at night to steal sugar beets in the fields, I refused to allow Erika to go with them. "Why not? He doesn't need them as much as we do. He has plenty," said the Pastor's wife. But I explained to Erika it was stealing, and she didn't go.

As the Pastor's wife, Frau Schwarz felt she had a God-given right to the pigeons in the church belfry. The flock belonged to the dovecotes of the Great House, again Herr Michel's property. But as they spent most of their time high in the belfry, even nesting there, the Schwarzes claimed them. It was the duty of delight for the older boys to climb up on the old rafters and catch them, and Erika often helped. At first she enjoyed the excitement and danger, but soon refused to go as she hated to see the pigeons killed.

On the edge of the fields on both sides of the village were rows of long, wooden barracks. They housed the Polish and Ukrainian forced laborers, women as well as men, who worked in the fields to replace the German laborers.[4] They

---

[4] In the spring of 1942, Germany had begun to take men and women between the ages of fifteen and sixty from occupied countries to replace German workers who had moved into the military or war-related industries. Eventually, there were 20,000 forced labor camps across the Reich, as well as marketplaces where businessmen and farmers could "buy" workers from Eastern countries. Legally, the workers were supposed to wear a special badge, "OST" ("East" for Eastern worker), on the right side of their chests to identify them, but Mary Jentsch makes no mention of such badges, perhaps because, like many other laws, this one was ignored in the countryside.

must have been there at least a year, and a number of babies had been born in the barracks. Under Inspektor Hecker, two overseers had charge of these unfortunate people. Both these men were kinder than Herr Hecker himself, but the lot of the Slavs was a miserable one at best. They were entirely at the mercy of the overseer, and their treatment depended on his character, so their wellbeing varied enormously in different communities. Life wasn't as bad in Barnimskunow as in the neighboring villages of Warnitz and Waitendorf. But they suffered from cold in winter, with inadequate clothing and shoes and food. The Ukrainians tended to be better liked than the Poles, but most of the villagers were kind to the prisoners and often gave them old clothing and a bit of extra food. Poles and Germans had been traditional enemies, and there had been border skirmishes between the two wars. Here in the East near the Polish border, the bitterness was great.

* * * * * *

The food rationing system in Germany was extraordinarily competent, though extremely complicated, especially for the storekeeper. Farmers who produced the food had the largest rations. Laborers, both farm and factory, next. The order of precedence began with young babies, who received the most milk and vitamins; young children up to three were in the next category; those from three to seven, as I remember, in another; and those from seven to twelve received increasingly less milk, but more margarine and meat. The very old had meager rations, but more *gries* and a little white bread, which was very scarce. Pregnant women received special rations, but women between eighteen and sixty-five, who were not doing heavy labor, got less of everything, which was reasonable. Lemons and oranges had disappeared altogether in 1941. After 1943 there was no white flour. Each year, as the war went on, there were fewer categories for children, and after the spring of 1944 only young babies received milk. And, of course, medicines of all kinds were strictly rationed.

The system was admirable in its strict fairness, and the essentials were doled out regularly. If a certain amount of meat or margarine was due you that month, it was always forthcoming. Black marketeering was kept down by horrifying penalties: imprisonment and, rarely, even death. But it could not be entirely wiped out, especially in the country where it was harder to control. The farmers were the worst offenders, but they were not dealt with as harshly as the shopkeepers.

The Poles and Ukrainians had special ration cards, receiving much less meat, fat, and sugar than the German workers and no luxuries. The system worked differently in the city than in the country. In the first years of the war, luxuries such as an occasional tin of sardines, a quarter of a pound of real coffee, a jar of jam, would appear from time to time in the city food shops, unrationed. This was a sop to the grumbling Berliners. Such treats we never saw in the country, but we fared much better on the whole with more vegetables and fruit.

One of my duties was to go to Stargard once a week to get the vegetable ration for the whole household. Vegetables were not obtainable at Durre's or in any other city or village store, only in open markets. I'd leave fairly early in the morning to catch the seven o'clock train—the only morning train—with thirteen ration cards and four large string bags.

Stargard was a beautiful old market town with Gothic buildings: churches, guildhalls, towers, and gates dating from the Hansa era when the Ihne, flowing into the Oder, had been navigable for medieval ships. Now the little river just meandered dreamily through the picturesque streets.

I took my stand in the market place, pleasant enough in summer with its big trees, but bitter cold in the winter. It took all morning to fill my bags, and often I'd have to wait for more vegetables to come into town in the afternoon. I dreaded the days when cabbages were on display, so heavy and awkward they felt like croquet balls bumping my legs when I walked back tired from the station to Barnimskunow. I usually got as many as possible, five or six. The red cabbage was the best—with its sour-sweet sauce speckled with cumin seed, to eat with a roast pork, venison, goose, wild hare—while the other cabbages were used for sauerkraut, soups, and slaw.

Sometimes Frau Schwarz would go into Stargard with me, and then, after our marketing was done, we made a holiday of it. We made a round of the few shops open to try and get some of the necessities—stockings and underwear for the children, shoestrings, thread, darning cotton, a pot or pan or dish—anything that we could find. All these things grew scarcer and scarcer with every month, until by 1944 there was literally nothing we could spend money on but food and fuel. Clothing and household articles were rationed, but there simply ceased to be any. The only shoes now obtainable were wooden clogs, wooden sandals, and a very occasional pair of felt carpet slippers. We used clogs entirely outdoors, and in winter the felt carpet slippers were the only way we could keep our feet warm on the cold floors. The children had outgrown their clothes, which were worn out anyway, but stockings were our greatest problem. They were rarely obtainable and no good when we got them. Every mother spent hours a day darning with poor cotton until the stockings were practically "new" ones.

There was only one train back, late in the afternoon. Frau Schwarz and I would eat our *Butterbrot* in the square and after our shopping go to Frau Pastor Lemmke (the sister-in-law of my friend Frau Schwandt in Berlin), for a pleasant rest and a cup of real coffee. Our hostess supplied a roll or a slice of cake, and Frau Schwarz always brought enough coffee for two cups each for the three of us. This was a real treat to us all, and we savored it in Fran Lemmke's faded but agreeable library. (Frau Schwarz always managed to have a small amount of real coffee on hand by barter and trade and was very generous with me.) This Stargard pastor and his wife were a pleasant, bookish, elderly couple and I always enjoyed them, though he was rarely there.

Sometimes, we went on a real spree. The movies! One of us would queue up and the other hold seats at a nearby café. If all the tickets were gone before our turn, we'd both sit in the café and drink a cup of ersatz coffee and watch the great world around us. The café was always crowded. There we relaxed and felt young and adventurous. Sometimes Frau Schwarz produced a couple of battered cigarettes, and we felt quite sophisticated, sipping our nasty brew and flourishing our fags [slang for cigarettes]. Everything is relative, and the Stargard cafe served us as well as the Café de la Paix. Our debonair air often attracted a soldier or two, and they'd sit and talk with us. Frau Schwarz was at her best with men, and we heard a good deal of war news, especially after the defeats in the East. If we got into the movies, we always had to leave in the middle to catch the last train home. We never saw the end of any film, but this never deterred us.

Pyritz (pronounced Pure-ritz) to the south of us was a much smaller and sleepier town, and we occasionally went foraging there, hoping for some find in the way of stockings. On the same railroad line but in the opposite direction from Stargard, it was about ten miles from our station. One fine summer's day when I just missed the train, I walked, taking a dirt cart track through a fringe of wood that wandered more or less parallel with the railroad. It was shady and dappled with the early morning sunlight. I met only two carts and enjoyed the wide sky with puffy little clouds, the bees, and the silence. It took me five and a quarter hours to reach Pyritz, but why not? I came back late in the afternoon by train with some shoelaces and a length of clothesline, but I had had a lovely day all by myself.

On the train, which was almost empty, I found five or six English P.O.W.s with their German guard. I sat down beside one, and we began talking in English. The guard came to stop me, but I told him I was American and hadn't had a chance to speak English for years. He muttered but went back to the platform and didn't bother us again. They had been to the town below Pyritz to the dentist, and they told me the Allies were winning, and the war would soon be over. When I got off, one gave me a package of cigarettes. This encounter seemed unreal and was quite unsettling. But I had had an adventure and a present, and, exhausted as I was when I finally got home, my day had been memorable.

However monotonous the life in Barnimskunow, we had more and better food than we could have had in Berlin or Silesia. The Russians were still confining their bombing raids to the German army in the East. But the Allies were hammering at Berlin day and night. Barnimskunow lay some

120 miles from Berlin, and we felt the bombs strike at every raid. The ground trembled, the windows rattled violently and often shattered. We never understood why, though Stettin and Peenemunde were about forty miles from us, we felt the Berlin raids much more strongly, though in a big raid we could hear the Stettin bombs fall. A different geological formation, I expect.

Almost every night, late, when the village was asleep and our children, too, I would go to the small living room, and Frau Schwarz would turn on the BBC. It was a serious offense to listen to the enemy, and if we had been caught it would have gone badly for both of us. We listened all during the winter and got a fairly accurate picture, along with the daily German news, which always gave the facts even though colored with propaganda. We heard about the defeats, too, eventually. Frau Schwarz passed on the BBC news to trustworthy friends who didn't dare listen themselves. She also informed the soldiers home on leave of the news in broad *Pommersche Sprache* (diction) that delighted them. We were sure Herr Schultz would catch us some night and denounce us. I think he knew.

* * * * * *

During those first weeks in Pomerania I was so busy getting used to the Parsonage and the strange new life—and the early fall was so taken up with putting up and preserving the fruits of the harvest—that I had no time for social life. But as the days began to shorten, my social life began.

Frau Schwarz's ruthlessness was tempered by some very likeable traits. She had a capacity for unbounded warmth, loyalty, and generosity toward her real friends. And she was generally quick to forgive, if not forget. She was devoted to Else Wegener, who lived adjacent to us, and very dependent on her for congenial company. Else was fond of her, too, and understood her.

After the supper chores were over and the children in bed, Frau Schwarz would suddenly say, "Come along, Frau Jentsch, we'll go over to Frau Wegener's for a moment." We were always made welcome and sat cozily in her living room with a cup of hot tea. Else looked like a Holbein portrait. She was tall and big-boned, held herself very erect, her graying hair parted in the middle and drawn back straight and severe into a knot. Though she was not strictly handsome, her strong features showed great character, and she radiated good humor, intelligence and warmth. She wore dresses or blouses with a narrow, high collar that suited her but made her seem older, and her skirts were much longer than was fashionable. She was about fifty then.

As the winter wore on, we went to visit two or three times a week. Later Else told me she knew well enough why Frau Schwarz came so often—for the tea, and because Else had found in a dusty store cupboard a supply of pre-World War I cheap cigarettes. Sometimes she gave us each two per visit but no more, as the supply was not unlimited. We all enjoyed our evenings, gossiping, discussing the German official news, the BBC news, rumors, everything. As abruptly as we had come, Frau Schwarz would get up and leave.

Before long she became jealous of my growing friendship with Frau Wegener and found a most effective way of assuring that I did not visit Else without her. Frau Schwarz kept a police dog named Sita chained all day to the porch post. Sita was so wild and savage that only Frau Schwarz could feed or handle her. At night, after we were all indoors, she turned her loose to protect the house and orchard she said. No one else had a watchdog, and Sita was the terror of the village. Sita was outside when we went to Frau Wegener's, but with Frau Schwarz to command her, we were safe. Encountering Sita as I returned from a solitary visit to Else's convinced me not to try it again.

Frau Schwarz's most intimate friend in the neighborhood was a young widow with a twelve-year-old daughter. Owner of the estate at Warnitz, Frau Schoenfeld was as pretty, feminine, and gracious as Frau Schwarz was homely, masculine, and brusque. But they seemed to be devoted friends and held long gossipy telephone conversations.

Frau Schwarz's greatest pleasure was to go to Warnitz for Sunday supper. I was invited several times and enjoyed it thoroughly. In good weather we walked the two miles gladly; but in foul, Frau Schoefeld sent her Frenchman with a stylish horse and buggy for us. He was a P.O.W. from the Bordeaux wine region, where he owned a small vineyard. He worked on the Warnitz estate as gardener, handyman, and as coachman when a horse could be spared. He liked Frau Schoenfeld, and she treated him very well. After the war I heard from Frau Schwarz that they still corresponded.

Those evenings in Warnitz were like stepping into a Jane Austen novel. The house was a typical late eighteenth-century, North German manor house, simple rather than stately, but well proportioned and light and airy. A long, broad, red-tiled hall led through the house with an entrancing view of espaliered fruit trees against the old red brick wall. A cross-corridor opened at one end into a kitchen garden and at the other into a small, formal garden. It was a sunny country house with Beidermeir furniture and good rugs, charming and liveable. There were always five or six other guests, neighboring gentry, mostly elderly. How good the food tasted, laid out on a polished table with simple elegance! These landowners still had hams and excellent sausages hanging in their smoke houses, and when Frau Schoenfeld had a little party, we had the works. Once we had smoked breast of goose and smoked salmon. A good wine, fresh salad, cheese and fruit from her garden topped it off. We were a long way in time and place from Berlin.

Frau Pastor always strode into the drawing room in her high, black, polished boots, wearing the same severely-tailored, broadcloth suit, which she had made from evening clothes belonging to her husband. The gentry considered her a character and made allowances for her oddities because she was witty and entertaining, though they thoroughly disapproved of her. An audience stimulated her, and she always had the latest Hitler joke ready. As the guests were all old friends, everyone talked freely about the situation on the Eastern front and Hitler's suicidal policy.

We went home refreshed in every way.

When Frau Schoenfeld's *Inspektor* had been called to the Army, the government had sent a new one, whom she could neither control nor get rid of. He was rough to the Russians and Poles on the place, and she was constantly at war with him. Frau Schwarz would give her advice daily by phone on how to deal with him. Finally Frau Schwarz unearthed a past scandal, and Frau Schoenfeld was able to fire him.

Our other social outlet lay about a mile and a half east of the village at Waitendorf, where an older couple named Bernhard lived on a large and beautiful estate. We were not as intimate with them as with Frau Schoenfeld. They were a bit grander, but they, too, needed company at times; and Frau Schwarz was always ready and conveniently near at hand. She was invited to Sunday supper and to play cards with Herr Bernhard, who had been crippled by a fall from his horse. After a good supper (much less lavish than at Warnitz) set out on a long, oak, refectory table in a great baronial hall overlooking a stately terrace, the Bernhards, their niece, and Frau Schwarz settled down to *Scharkskopf*, an old game played with German cards which contain a whole hierarchy of royal faces.

I retired to a small and elegant parlor with Frau General Bernhard. She was the charming Dutch wife of Herr Bernhard's brother, a general on the Eastern front. We liked each other at once and spoke in nostalgic French of pre-war Paris, England, and Switzerland. She had two sons in the army (one later reported missing and never heard of again) and the Waitendorf Bernhards had four (two of them were killed). Frau General Bernhard was visiting Waitendorf, hoping to see her husband, who was trying to get a couple of days' leave and join her.

The next time I went to Waitendorf, the General was there, having arrived unexpectedly for a twenty-four-hour visit. I was impressed by his quiet charm. He naturally didn't say much in my presence, but we gathered the situation in the East was already grim. It was obvious they all distrusted the Nazi regime and considered Hitler and his leaders fanatical and dangerous fools.[5] But as a German and a gen-

---

[5] By the end of 1943 many among the German high command were aware that the war was being lost. In July of that year, the Russians had launched their first summer offensive against German troops. In July and August, the U.S. had carried out the devastating bombings of Hamburg; in September, the Allies landed in Italy and though German troops continued to occupy much of the country, the Italians signed an armistice. In November, there was a large British air raid on Berlin. Hitler's insistence that the German army operate on two and eventually three fronts was weakening its position on all of them.

eral, he wanted the German army to win. Later the General was hanged in Krakow by the Poles. It is strange to think of someone you have met in a drawing room "hanged by the neck." I have often wondered what became of the General's wife. I doubt if she could or would go back to Holland.

We usually came home about midnight. There was not a glimmer of light over the entire countryside, and it was quite spooky. One of the things hard to imagine unless one has lived in war-ridden Europe is the effect of an all-out blackout. It was much worse in the cities, Berlin especially, as there were so many hazards: falling over curbs, down steps, losing one's direction. There were fewer accidents in the country, and most people went to bed early and stayed indoors at night. But when you were outdoors, the blackness was total and seemed to deepen the absolute silence of the country night. Any tiny noise was intensified and frightening. Frau Schwarz and I clumped home in the blackness, swinging the big sticks we carried for protection, our metal-rimmed heels occasionally striking stones with a sharp metallic ring that startled us. We were always relieved to get past the sinister barracks and to find Sita at the edge of our village. After these pleasant forays into a more civilized world, our daily life seemed dull and primitive.

Frau Wegener was never invited to visit the local gentry. They all liked, admired, and respected her, and they all exchanged news and gossip with her over the counter of her store. Frau Bernhard even had long social telephone conversations with her on some business pretext, but they never invited her to their homes. She was the daughter of a farmer-storekeeper-innkeeper and therefore ineligible to enter that closed, feudal society, though her family was an old one and both she, her sister, and her husband were educated people. She would have added greatly to their pleasure, especially in war-time, when everyone was so isolated by the lack of transportation. I resented their attitude toward Else, and later when we became good friends, we sometimes spoke of it. She shrugged her shoulders; it had always been so and always would be. She minded it more for the children's sakes, particularly for her daughter, Eva, who had been well educated at a boarding school.

One of my more unpleasant memories of that winter of 1943-44 was my series of trips to the dentist in Stargard. There were only two dentists left in that town. At last I got an appointment, which I soon found meant nothing. Of course I had to take the 6:45 a.m. train, as there was no other. Arriving in town about seven, I stood in line in the cold, outside the office until it opened at 8:30. Unfortunately the Stargarders had an edge on me as they could get there by six if they wished, and many did. Sometimes there were a dozen people waiting when I arrived. When the assistant came and opened the door, she took down our names in the order of the line. I soon learned the discouraging truth: if I were too far down the line, I would have to wait for the afternoon session. Even then, if a soldier on leave or a nurse came along, they were taken before the rest of us. Twice I went back to Barnimskunow without having sat in the dentist's chair.

But waiting in queues at the market place was often amusing. We women would stand chattering and stamping our feet in the cold for an hour and along would come a soldier on leave. He had the right to crowd in ahead of us and shop for his wife or mother—if he dared. But often our vociferous clamor intimidated him.

Not so the pregnant women. They were entitled to

first place, but they had to run the gauntlet. "Where's your card?" someone would shout. "You aren't pregnant; prove it." Or, "Look here, my girl, your husband hasn't been back since September—I know that for a fact—so who is he?" Sometimes the young woman indignantly produced her pregnancy card, and there was a shout of approval: "Let her through." The more sedate matrons shook their heads in disapproval at this display of vulgarity.

* * * * * *

One noon, just before dinner, Frau Pastor came rushing from the radio, her face set and her eyes intense. "*Kinder, Kinder*," she called in a low hoarse whisper so charged with drama that every child heard it and came swiftly from all corners of the house.

"*Halle ist gebombed—total gebombed—bis zum letzte Haus. Tante Marthe ist bestimmt tot.*" This latter in a deep sepulchral voice. (Halle has just been bombed—totally—to the last house. Aunt Martha is certainly dead.)

I was horrified, and Erika and Jerry ready to burst into tears until the word *bestimmt* (certainly) hit my ears again. Just gruesome speculation to create drama! We got used to the same scene with variations whenever Dresden, Leipzig, and other cities were bombed. There seemed always to be a near relative who was *bestimmt tot* in each one. When first one, and then a second of Frau Schwarz's younger brothers were killed at the front, I had to be convinced that it was true.

Jerry and I staged a real if minor drama one wintry day when the sun came out after a storm and sparkled on the snow. I pulled him to the store on a little sled to get our month's supplies of staples. I had the ration cards of all thirteen of us. I carried out the heaviest things first, among them a ten-pound sack of sugar. This I put for safety in Jerry's lap. When I came out again I got a shock that nearly made me faint. He and the sled and the snow around were covered with rapidly melting sugar! His legs and arms clasped around the precious burden were wet, and the sack had disintegrated. More than three-quarters of the sugar was gone. Trembling, I scraped up what little I could rescue. Nothing more awful could have happened. Not only our small ration, but the sugar of ten other people was lost. Neither money nor love could replace it.

There was nothing to do but to brave Frau Schwarz and Herta. There was a scene, but Frau Schwarz behaved better than I had expected. Else Wegener came to the rescue, as she usually did, and gradually made up at least five pounds, and I turned over our ration cards to the household for the next two months. It was a tale long told in the village, Puppe inventing so many lurid details—my beating Jerry until he had bleeding welts, and no puddings in the family for six months—that Jerry became a sort of doubtful hero.

But he was a real one to the village children in our next drama. One day someone, probably Ernst-Wilhelm, let Sita loose in the house. I heard screams and rushed out of the sitting-room to see Puppe, Erika, Jürgen, and Jerry streaking down the long corridor for dear life, Sita after them. Jerry was last, and in their excitement the other children got through a door and slammed it shut. Sita got Jerry in the seat of his pants and was rescued by Frau Schwarz just in time. He was scared but not hurt.

Soon after we arrived at the rectory, I took charge of Schwesterchen (the smallest Schwartz). Crista was a sweet

child, and we were all very fond of her. Every night at bed-
time the nursery was cleared, the big plank table wiped off,
and we brought in two great washtubs and buckets of hot
and cold water. I bathed Crista, then Jerry and Erika, in the
small tub, while Herta scrubbed Jürgen, Puppe, and then
saw to it that Christian and Ernst-Wilhelm scrubbed the
mud and manure off themselves properly. It was bedlam—
such clatter, chatter, sputtering, splashing. Herta was cheerful and efficient, though she had a rough hand. She stood no
nonsense from Puppe or Ernst-Wilhelm.

There was endless work for all the grown-ups. Frau
Schwarz tended the vegetable garden and helped with the
cooking, canning, and the big wash, which here we did
weekly. I helped with preparing the vegetables, looking after
Schwesterchen, and often washed the dishes, with Christian,
Erika, and Puppe drying them. We all did what was most
urgent at the moment. Evenings we patched and darned the
children's clothes.

After the sugar-beet harvest in late summer, Frau Pastor, like Lehrer Schultz and the cottagers, got her share of
beets from the estate and begged more from Frau Bernhard.
(She also traded some few of her rarer apples to Frau Bernhard for a quantity of grain for her pigs, chickens, turkeys,
and geese, of which she kept more than her allotment, hiding them successfully when an inspector came around.) She
borrowed a hand beet-press, and we rolled up our sleeves
and set to making syrup. The kitchen was in a sticky tur-
moil for several days, but it was fun all working together.
First the great white beets, as large as small cabbages and
hard as stones, had to be peeled. Peel is the wrong word:
their rough exterior had to be hacked off with strong, sharp
knives. Herta, Anna, and Frau Schwarz cut them as they cut

bread loaves, toward themselves.

After the beets were finally all cut into pieces, they were put into an enormous cauldron of boiling water on the stove, one batch at a time. Each batch simmered for about two hours, and in rotation each cauldron-full was skimmed off three times. At last all the different pails of final skimmings were poured together into the cauldron and let simmer until they reached the requisite thickness and color, a light brown. The mash was given to the pigs and goats. We feasted off the syrup all winter, and the children loved it on bread. It was a great saving on sugar, which grew scarcer every month, so that most of it could go into preserving.

The children all seemed healthy; not many colds and no epidemics had struck us. But we began to notice that any scratch got infected, and the children were constantly getting scratches. It took them a long time to heal, and as soon as they got over one infection, another appeared. We soon got used to seeing them with sores all over their legs and arms. In spite of our seemingly good and abundant diet, it consisted mostly of carbohydrates. There was an increasing lack of vitamins and minerals and certainly not enough milk and fat.[6]

Early in March, I stuck a needle in my finger. It got infected and Schwester Elfrieda, the rural district nurse who came twice a week to Barnimskunow, treated it. A day or two later I stuck a pin in my index finger. The first finger looked so red and ugly that I paid little attention to the other, un-

---

[6] A letter that Gerhard, who was still working on the library in Beeskow, sent to Erika in February 1944, must have appealed to both her imagination and hunger. He wrote: "Ripe fish hang on the trees along the River Spree and the children have a holiday to help pick them....The marzipan fields can already be harvested. And leprechauns strew peas every evening."

til one night Frau Schwarz happened to come in my room after I had gone to bed to tell me something. She suddenly saw my arm. "Frau Jentsch, your arm!" There were three red streaks to my elbow. "Blood poison!" she said dramatically. She called the nearest doctor eight kilometers away, and he told her my arm must be kept up all night and that I was to come to him next morning by nine o'clock. He was only allowed enough gas for his car for emergencies.

Next morning Erika wanted to go with me; Jerry too, but he was too little. We set out after a quick cup of ersatz coffee and bread. It was a cold, windy March morning, and the walk seemed endless, with my arm over my head and throbbing. Dr. Marseilles examined my finger, and it did look pretty awful, swollen and encrusted with a completely hard black shell. "Why didn't you come before?" he growled.

He called his wife and sister, sent Erika outside to play, and while Frau Marseilles held my arm rigid and her sister held the other arm, he cut the nasty crust, and then the flesh off the top of my finger and both sides down to the bone. He had no local anesthetic or pain killer to waste on such a minor operation at this stage of the war. I survived without fainting, and he told me to go home and bathe it six times a day in the hottest water I could stand with plenty of common laundry soap, and to call him in a few days. This treatment was an agony, but it healed surprisingly quickly and I didn't even lose my nail.

Our relations with the Schwarzes became more and more strained during the long confined winter. The children were indoors more, there was more ganging up on Erika and Jerry, and more of Puppe's outrageous lies. Also Frau Schwarz was pregnant, and she and I lost our tempers frequently, generally over the children. One day I broke one of her grandmother's old and very best coffee cups. It couldn't be replaced, even by a cheap one, but she made a scene out of all proportion to the cause. I think she was getting tired of us in her house, usurping her dining room and her privacy and eating her food, as food grew ever scarcer. The rent and board I paid her would have been adequate in normal times, but now money was practically worthless. You could buy nothing with it but rationed food. She also became more and more nervous and restless as the war and her pregnancy wore on.

This all culminated in a fearful episode. One day after dressing Schwesterchen, who had just awakened from her nap, I put her down on her feet and had just reached for a diaper on the floor when she took a step, lost her balance, and fell hard against the sharp corner of a bureau. She lay perfectly still. I was petrified. I called Herta and then everyone came running. When I picked her up she looked lifeless, but blood was spurting from her forehead.

Frau Schwarz snatched her from me. Then, "You've killed Crista, you've killed my baby!" The whole clan took up the cry, "Frau Jentsch has killed Schwesterchen!" I really thought I had. Then the baby began to scream, and we realized she was alive. Only Herta remained calm and soothed the child. She soon stopped crying and her color came back. She was uninjured except for a bad gash on her forehead (which did, unfortunately, leave a white scar).

I said how sorry I was, but no one heeded me in the general melodrama. Finally, "You're never to touch her again!" Frau Schwarz told me. I answered that I never wanted to; that it was a simple accident that could have happened to anyone, and that I did not feel I had been negligent. I repeated that I was sorry, and that I was very fond of Crista, but I did not feel it warranted such a scene. By that time the children had roused the neighbors, and Else came over. She and the other women told Frau Schwarz she was making an unseemly furor, which only incensed her more.

* * * * * *

I went over to Else's that afternoon and told her I wouldn't stay at the Parsonage any longer. She agreed with me, but pointed out that she knew of no room available anywhere, and that I had better wait. In a few days she had miraculously arranged with Frau Hecker, the *Inspektor's* wife, to give me a small room in her house. Although the farm with its many outbuildings was large, she already had many other refugees, but I think she agreed to take me partly because she disliked Frau Schwarz. We couldn't board with them and certainly would not get the extra food we had been having, but nothing mattered to me now but to leave the *Pfarrhaus* and the intolerable situation there.

We were settled in a corner of the *Gutbesitzer's Hof* within a week. Frau Schwarz and I were no longer speaking, ridiculous in a small village with only one street and one store! As it turned out, we didn't meet often as her children did all the errands; also Frau Pastor and Frau Hecker never darkened each other's doors. The situation was hardest on Frau Wegener. She had so few contacts on her own level—none but Frau Schwarz during the confinement of the war—and now because she had helped me, she was cut off from this one congenial contact. It was all a tempest in a teapot, but at the time it seemed as turbulent as a tornado in the tropics.

In spite of less food, the children were happier. Friedgard Hecker was Erika's age and in her class. She was a big, rather pretty, dark girl, conventional and dull like her mother and completely under the latter's domination. Annelise, nicknamed Vivey, was younger than Erika by a year, but the two became great friends. Vevey was light and quick and imaginative like Erika, and they had great scope for inventive games in the park and gardens and the great *Hof*. Jerry played with Bubi (Oskar) Hecker, younger and not as congenial as Jürgen Schwarz, but still quite satisfactory. Their joy was to tear up and down the labyrinth of long brick corridors on their tricycles. By now Jerry's rubber tires had rotted off, and one of Herr Hecker's friendly gestures was to have the rims straightened and filled in with wooden "tires." They also played in the *Hof* and park.

The one serious difficulty was that Friedgard and her mother were jealous of Erika's preference for Vevey. Frau Hecker was obtuse enough to tell me that as Freidgard was the same age as Erika, and in her class, they should always play together! Friedgard was her mother's favorite. Vevey was too flighty and unladylike, and Erika abetted her. I paid no attention, of course, only to stipulate that they sometimes include Friedgard.

It was curious and almost incredible that in that tiny village with just one street, our move to the Heckers', within sight of and only five minutes walk from the Parsonage, was into a different world. We might have been a hundred miles away. We were involved with a completely new set of people, in completely new surroundings, and had a different routine. Except in school, Erika and Jerry saw nothing of the Schwarzes.

We had a small room with a porcelain stove for heating.

It was dark because the two windows gave on to a wide, vine-covered verandah overlooking the shadiest part of the park. It was quite cold and damp in winter and had a brick floor. One long ell of the house was entirely given up to the Hecker's great kitchen facing the *Hof*, and then a long series of kitchen pantries, storerooms, the buttery, the preserve room, the stillroom, and a great room where the smoked meats hung—rows of hams, spare ribs, and delectable sausages, long and thin, short and fat, hard and soft. These rooms all looked out into the big, well-kept poultry yard. Beyond the meat room were the laundry and then three sunny little rooms at the very end of the long ell, sunny because the windows looked out on the kitchen gardens. These had been made into makeshift kitchens for the refugees with little iron stoves, plank tables, and several chairs.

Characteristically, Frau Hecker shifted a couple of families into one and insisted on giving to me alone the end room, the brightest. There we reigned in solitary splendor. It was unfair, but I was grateful. On rainy days we could sit in there, and I could darn and mend while Erika and Jerry drew or read or did their homework. It was a real break after the confusion and noise of the Parsonage kitchen. Indeed, the quiet and the independence more than made up for all the material advantages we had lost.

I was entranced by the bustle and variety of the life of the estate, a beehive of activity. The better I knew it, the more it seemed like the feudal pattern of the Middle Ages: the castle, with its busy courtyards, the "serfs" outside the walls toiling in the fields—everything but the moat and drawbridge. These big estates were practically self-sufficient. Everyone had his place in the scheme, usually handed down from father to son, and everyone was busy. There was a cheerful bustle in good weather, which was even reflected in the Poles and Ukrainians. In peacetime it must have been a satisfying and even rewarding life for everyone, not excepting the lowliest farmhand. Perhaps I am romanticizing. Many of the younger generation must have resented their utter dependence on the *Gutsbesitzer* and the overseer, but when I was there, they were all gone to war.

These *Guts* were as different as possible to any type of American farm or ranch. Perhaps they were most like the ante-bellum Southern plantations in their self-sufficiency, and yet diversified as the old New England small farm. Their output, even in normal times, was prodigious. Nothing was wasted, cultivation was intense, methods and management modern and efficient, keeping just enough of the old to balance the new. Perhaps the real secret was the human element. It is natural to Germans to work hard. The estates I saw were exploited to the nth degree—crops, cattle, humans—and hummed with activity from sunup to sundown. Since the sugar-beet fields had replaced the acres of waving grain, a toy railroad ran through the fields where the beets were loaded in little cars to expedite the harvest.

Our street came in from the west in a long straight line from the Warnitz road, made a sharp right angle northward, and then another continuing sharp east to the Waitendorf road. The *Hecker Gut* was at this second angle, extending west and north of Barnimskunow. At the left of the street was the big oak gate to the estate with high brick walls enclosing the property along both sides of the corner. Inside the gates (which were closed and locked at night with a little door for humans on one side), a vast rectangular yard spread out, cobbled in patterns, with a swept and garnished look in spite of the incessant activity of men and beasts. In the middle was a large grassy circle outlined with shade trees, and beyond a smaller one. On the right, set back in a small lawn with shrubs, was the large country house, with its gardens, orchards and park behind it, to the north. At the left of the gate were the great cow barns with a cobbled runway leading to the watering troughs, and beyond to a small pond with thick brown liquid running into it via a spillway from an upper story of an old brick distillery.

Schnapps was distilled here from the sugar beets, but during the war only for the army. The big herd of Holstein dairy cows drank this waste daily, and I was told it was their chief food now. The cow pastures had been ploughed into beet fields, and the cows only left their barns to walk around the *Hof* twice a day and drink at the pond. Nevertheless, they seemed healthy and the milk was good.

Behind the distillery to the south was a lane with the smithy, the leather and harness shop, the carpenter shop, and the general repair shed. Opposite the gate and beyond the grass circles were the horse stables and barns, the carriage shed, the cart and wagon sheds, and the hay barns. There were few horses now, only one pair of carriage horses and one riding horse for Herr Hecker and the overseers.

Behind these, to the right, were two paddocks, a small pasture and the great, round, stone silo, hoary with age and moss, a somewhat sinister-looking place. Then came the pig sties and wallows, and last, the sheep folds and the dipping runs. To the right of the house on the kitchen side was a big modern poultry yard, Frau Hecker's pride, with handsome geese, turkeys, ducks, chickens, and guinea fowl. These were sadly depleted because of the present grain regulations, and she had to sell most of them and their eggs to the local government. Indeed, the chickens now were the main stock;

the others were considered luxuries, as they certainly were. The fowl and eggs were counted regularly by a government inspector and collected on schedule to be sold in local or city markets. This was also true of all the cattle and other farm produce.

A high wall to the north separated the park, orchard, and vegetable gardens from the fields. As all the able-bodied men had long since gone to war, the field work was done by the Ukrainians and Poles, but the more skilled jobs, such as the blacksmithing and stable work, was still manned by a few Germans, old men and boys. The Polish and Russian women and girls with the help of native girls milked and tended the cows.

This *Gut* was really a busy village. It was a paradise for the children, and we all three grew absorbed in its daily life. Night and morning we went to get our own milk. The children's milk rations were now small, but every now and then we got an extra dollop in our pail as protégés of Frau Hecker. It was a perilous journey into the cow barn. The planks along the mud floor between the rows of cows were slippery and narrow, and the children often fell off into the bovine mire. Then there was the ever-present probability of a cow lifting her tail and spattering us. But we loved it. It was so cozy on cold winter mornings and evenings among the warm, steamy beasts with the good smell of warm milk. Our butter and cheese we bought at Durre's store like everyone else.

Herr Michels, our *Gutbesitzer*, had never seen fit to modernize the Hecker's kitchen. The only water for the whole house was a pump. Though the handle was within the house, for some reason it always had to be started up on the outside, which in winter meant someone going out in the cold every time we needed water. (Frau Schwarz's pump was all inside, and Frau Wegener had running water in her house.)

But the Hecker kitchen was a fascinating place. Huge, with a great iron, wood-burning stove with a blackened canopy, and a battery of enormous copper pots, pans and utensils strung around the wall, it was the busiest and most cheerful room in the house. There was an old earthen baking oven in the center and big deal [a term for cheap wood] tables in two rows along the walls. Frau Hecker supervised her household while two women helpers did all the work (some of the *Hof* men were fed there). Both Frau Wegener and Frau Schwarz had told me that she was a very poor housekeeper: she couldn't organize, was chicken-headed, and made a great fuss scolding and doing nothing. She and her husband were both well known for being miserly. She could have given us a great deal more than she did in the way of meat and vegetables and fruit, though according to her lights she was generous. I was grateful for the extras she did dole out to us, always with a great air of secrecy, so as not to antagonize the other, less fortunate, refugees, who nevertheless always knew.

Herr Hecker's old aunt and uncle, a devoted brother and sister who lived there, were a sweet old couple, and though Frau Hecker made a great fuss over them, she was very stingy with them, too, and gave them very meager rations. I was quite fond of Tante and Onkel, as we all called them, and used to go to talk with them on the shady verandah or in Tante's room. She attended to most of the poultry work and did an excellent job, though her niece took the credit. She also did most of the family mending.

That second summer in Barnimskunow was very pleasant in spite of the now unceasing large-scale bombing of Stettin, Peenemunde (on the Baltic), and Berlin, which was already half destroyed. We now saw the Americans in operation, hundreds of tiny, silvery flying fish glinting in the sun, beautiful and remote and so harmless looking, flying high in the sky over us. We all ran out to see them and suddenly Jerry decided that his mythical Uncle Bob (my brother), whom he had never seen, was leading this magnificent parade in the sky, and so would not think of dropping bombs on us. I quickly quashed this idea before it spread to the village children, since it was not calculated to make us too popular. The United States seemed as remote as Mars now; I had been completely cut off for three years.

Though daily life was simple, it was hard work and took twice as long as in normal times or in a less primitive place. My kitchen stove was recalcitrant, the water pails were heavy, and I was responsible for scrubbing two long corridors twice a week. There was another pump in the *Hof* and several in the village. As the kitchen pump was mostly for Frau Hecker's use, I had to draw two buckets, sometimes more, daily from the *Hof* for drinking, washing, cleaning, and scrubbing. For a short time that summer the *Hof* pump went dry, and I had to fetch and carry from the nearest one in the village—not far, but two pails of water are heavy, and the dirty water had to be carried out to empty.

Our rations dwindled perceptibly as time went on, but now that I was away from the Parsonage and on my own, Frau Wegener managed to smuggle me a substantial amount of staples from time to time: sugar, *Gries*, cheese, and a little tea. Margarine was harder to get as there was so little of it. But she very often gave me the delicious goose fat that she made into a spread. We mixed it with a little chopped onion, and salt and pepper, and it was very rich. When cold, it cut like butter, and the children loved it spread thinly on the good dark bread we had. These gifts had to be wangled out of the Wegeners' and Fraulein Lise's own rations in secret, for though the latter sometimes made me little presents, she would have been horrified at the extent of her sister's gifts. (As shopkeeper and farmers they had more rations than the ordinary citizens.) There was now never even one-third of the necessary soap, and the washing became more and more difficult. Some of the villages made soap, and once Frau Hecker made a batch and gave me a little.

When I first went to the Heckers', they invited me into their living room to sit and mend with them after the children were in bed. It was pleasant at first, a change from my own room, especially when Tante and Onkel were there, but they went to bed early. Herr Hecker, though friendly, was pompous with a false joviality, and Frau Hecker was dull. Besides, she soon began to nod over her darning. Once or twice he brought out some cordial, but I could see she disapproved.

Soon I began to slip over to Else's, diagonally across the street, almost every evening. We talked and talked over a good cup of tea: the story of our lives, our children, war rumors, gossip, everything. I felt I had known her for years. Sometimes Fraulein Lise came over from the big house, and this dampened our liveliness. She and Else had never got along very well and now their close daily proximity in the store aggravated it. Eva would often be around. There was nothing for her in the village, and she was lonely. Twelve-year-old Ernst, a quiet, sweet, hard-working little boy, lay in bed in the next room. He always left his door open a crack to hear us talk. On very special occasions Else produced a tiny glass of homemade cordial, and several times she triumphantly brought in a cup of delicious powdered coffee. It was nectar, and we savored that one cup for half an hour.

This became my haven, and it made life bearable. The Heckers were no substitute for Frau Schwarz, but Frau Wegener was far superior as a warm and congenial friend to anyone I had known in Germany. I didn't dare go every night, however, as the Heckers became offended. She told me she and her husband didn't understand how I could prefer Frau Wegener's company to their society. I didn't want to antagonize them, so I graced their living room at least once a week. I was amused, for they began to go intellectual on me and tried to impress me with their cultivated conversation. (I had to get a little gate key from Herr Hecker every time I went out at night, so they kept tabs on me!)

Sometimes in the summer days I took the children on long walks. I found a path leading beyond the fields to a low ridge, a little lane between rows of stunted willows, high above the fields. There we went along under the big sky, with only the larks soaring above us. Early in the morning or late in the afternoon was the best time to hear the cuckoos as they skimmed past, the clear monotonous call, so low and cool, of old English poetry. These walks were one of the things I like best to remember of our life in Pommern. I had begun to love the alien flat landscape, with its far horizons, its straight rows of old trees, and its soft low sky with fleecy little white clouds or great stormy purple ones. Pommern, too, was a fair land.

Late in the summer, we came upon flocks of sheep with their shepherds and dogs, flowing between the fields into the road. They had been gleaning the stubble after the beet harvest. Otherwise, like the cows, they had to stay confined in their pens. After the potato harvest we saw the men storing potatoes for the winter in long low mounds near the roads, each with its tiny wooden door at one end. They dotted the landscape like prehistoric barrows.

There was always something exciting going on in the *Hof*. One day, two veterinarians drove up and we learned that some young colts were to be gelded. Frau Hecker came flustering to me that the girls were to be kept out of the *Hof*. But I watched with interest, as did the boys and no doubt the girls from windows.

Six or seven glossy colts were led out into the big green circle. After they were tethered to the low fence, the first was thrown, and I believe an anesthetic was given. He was held down, gelded, and left to lie while the next one was thrown. They lay quite still for at least half an hour before they stirred and were allowed to get up. It all took about two hours before they were led back to their stalls. The vets (they were hard to come by now) spent the day seeing to the other stock and had lunch with Herr Hecker.

One unique aspect of our Pomeranian villages—and a noisy and entertaining one—was the geese. We had a great flock, some eight hundred or so. In peacetime their feet were dipped in tar for walking over cobblestones, and they were driven in great droves to Berlin for Christmas dinners. Each cottager owned five or six at least, and there were large populations at the Great House, Hecker's, Durre's, and the butcher's and baker's.

Early every morning a couple of girls, chosen as official goose-girls for the season, followed by two or three smaller ones, went the length of the street opening each cottage gate in turn. Each goose and gander was already waiting, cackling at its gate, and down the street with great noise and bickering waddled the flock, jostling for first place but soon settling into an orderly march. The girls drove them with long sticks out of the village and into one of several small pastures set aside for them. If it was in school term, the little girls would be left there all morning, eating their bread and butter with the geese. Late in the afternoon the goose-girls (Erika was very proud when she was initiated into that ancient profession) led them all home, first taking them for a splashing and some liquid refreshment in the village pond. Sometimes they spent half a day at the pond. Back in the street, each goose turned into its own yard proudly, without a prod, and immediately began to hiss defiantly. I decided they were the most intelligent of the domestic fowl. Better than watchdogs, they guarded their little yards with a most possessive zeal. Woe to any stranger entering the gate. I still have a scar on my leg from an inhospitable gander.

Jerry started school in August 1944, when he was almost six. He had to walk only a short distance from the Heckers' to the schoolhouse. The small boys often plagued the geese behind the closed yard gates, but sometimes the gates were left open, and one old gander, especially, took his revenge. He darted out with neck outstretched, hissing furiously, attacking his tormentors as they ran past. Jerry had several bites and so many narrow escapes that he refused to go alone, so for a while I had to escort him to school.

Magic was wrought one day that summer. Suddenly out of nowhere a fairy host came down our street: first two gay and graceful children on white horses, with colored trappings, then six tiny ponies stepping daintily, drawing a small, brightly-painted wagon. Looming behind, incredibly exotic, were two ponderous elephants, swirling the dust with their heavy yet delicate tread. Darting all around this procession frolicked a couple of waggish white dogs. A real circus! The children were all dumb for a moment with joy and amazement. I could not have been more surprised to see Cinderella in her coach descending upon us. To everyone's joy, they stopped at our *Hof* gate and after a short conference with Herr Hecker, who was hauled forth from his office by the children, they drove in and took possession of an empty horse barn and stable! He agreed to provide a stable for the ponies, barn for the elephants, and hay for all, following the immemorial custom of the country. In return, they were to give a performance a day, and two on Saturdays. The circus family slept in the loft.

Our circus was a bonanza out of the blue. It was slowly trekking west from East Prussia, begging hay and barns along the route. All the children living on Hecker's *Hof* claimed it as their especial property, and the Hecker children fairly strutted. It stayed over a week, and we knew the whole troupe intimately. The star was a bright, friendly girl of twelve, who with her younger brother went to school in the mornings. Our children watched them practice every day. She was an accomplished acrobat and bareback rider and obligingly tried to teach them some of her stunts. Erika and Vevey even rode rather clumsily through a hoop!

Every afternoon after school, they erected their tiny tent and gave a performance. It was an enchantment. Every child in the village, including the Russian and Polish, was at every performance, and so were all of the adults who could possibly be there. We helped curry the ponies and watched the two men, brothers, bathe and water the elephants. Erika and Jerry were quite proud of me when I astonished the men by my superior knowledge of the great beasts. I identified them as Indian elephants and not African! I told them of all the great circuses I had seen—Barnum and Bailey and Ringling—and could truthfully declare that none had ever pleased me more. But alas! The week was soon up, and the enchanting fairy tale vanished from our lives. Later, on our trek west, we passed several similar troupes, the poor little ponies plodding valiantly along the crowded roads, with the wagons stripped of all their gay circus panoply and no elephants, a sinister sign. We were all saddened by the sight.

There had always been hundreds of little family circuses wandering over the German countryside, and I was astonished that after five years of total war they were not yet disbanded, though certainly their numbers had decreased. It was a wise indulgence on the part of the Government, for the rural population had few distractions now, when lack of transportation isolated them more and more. In the cities and towns there were still movies, theatre, and concerts. And the ubiquitous hairdresser was allowed to ply her trade, using up precious electric power, to the very end, even in small towns like Pyritz and Stargard.

Several times Else took me to Stargard with her, and how different they were to my former marketing expeditions. We walked to the station in the fresh morning in a pleasurable spirit of adventure. After doing our marketing and "shopping"—perhaps some shoelaces made of tough paper, or some neat squares of old newspapers tied together as toilet paper—we ate our *Butterbrot* on a shady bench in the square and then walked across the Ihne past a great coal yard to a pleasant house beside it on the bend of the little river on the outskirts of town.

Here lived Else's cousins, the Stohrs, a hearty, prosperous coal dealer and his wife, a pretty, coquettish woman who liked clothes and antique furniture. We were made welcome, and Else proceeded to open her bag and take out a chicken, a half-pound of butter, or half a dozen eggs. The butter she always presented to Frau Stohr. Her main object in town was to trade the chicken or the eggs to some of the Frenchmen from the Stargard P.O.W. barracks, whom the coal dealer employed and with whom he was on good terms, for a little jar of powdered real coffee, sent them regularly by the Red Cross.

After Else had discreetly dispatched this business, Frau Stohr set out a little tea table laid with a white cloth and pretty Dresden china and produced two cups of coffee apiece—real bean coffee, freshly roasted, and a slice of cake or little ham and cucumber sandwiches, sometimes both, if Else's contribution had been large! This was very festive, and we chatted and duly admired our hostess's newest hairdo or the costume she had just made over from some old dress. We tried to sip our coffee as daintily and elegantly as she! It was a pleasant, inconsequential interlude, but a change from life at Barnimskunow. Else and I always enjoyed the trip back and forth together, and as we had no stimulants—no alcohol, cigarettes, coffee, or tea—these two cups of good strong coffee stimulated us like strong drink, soothed our nerves, and sent our spirits soaring.

Else also introduced me to several of her friends and protégées around the village, and later I called on them alone. The cottage rooms were all tiny, but neat and tidy and *gemütlich*. Such visits stood me in good stead. One woman was an accomplished seamstress, and, in return for some outgrown clothing of Erika's that even Jerry couldn't wear, she made Erika a skirt out of one outgrown dress and a slip from another. Later in the fall, with the prospect of winter ahead, Frau Wegener got me a length of heavy, navy-blue, nubbly cloth for a winter coat. It was horrid stuff (part cotton mixed with reprocessed wool, heavy rather than warm), but it was the only kind of cloth the government issued for coats. For variety, there was a choice of three colors: blue, black, or brown. The Government did issue another kind of cloth for suits and dresses, but that was all—and even this narrow selection was unprocurable in the country. Frau Wegener had managed to get the cloth through a friend in Berlin who had a wholesale goods business, and though it was ugly and took my saved-up ration card supplemented by some of Else's coupons, I was grateful. My ancient nutria jacket bought in Boston in 1923 was literally falling apart.

One of the uglier aspects of village life was the pig slaughtering, when the pig was strung up and its throat was slit. Jerry disappeared early in the morning and returned late. I don't know how much he saw, but it must have been pretty gory. I went out to find him when the pig was already hanging, his blood dripping into a great pot.

Later, I was called over to the Durres' to help with the sausage making after the slaughter. It was a busy scene and added to my country education. The hams and ribs were hung up to be smoked later, the loins and chops stored, the feet salted and pickled, the fat tied and salted, and the intestines emptied and carefully washed and cleaned for sausage cases. I am not sure what part of the hog was used for the various sausages, but it was chopped and mixed in big wooden bowls, each with different herbs for seasoning. Stuffing it into the intestines was a skilled job, and I wasn't allowed to tackle it until taught. There was a great variety of sausage, all to be smoked and hung, and some, the very hard kind, were smoked longer. Some of the softer ones, like liverwurst, were put in intestines and smoked, and others went into jars for use as a spread. The heart was kept to be eaten in the next few days. Last came the *Blutwurst*. The blood was mixed with some of the sausage meat, made into a soft mash with semolina or some other fine meal, boiled lightly, and eaten immediately. This was our reward for helping and our noonday meal. It looked horrible, but tasted very good.

One night early in that summer, we awoke to a loud explosion. Bombing! We couldn't believe it, but it was true. Several bombs had dropped in a plowed field just outside the village and had killed a boy returning from the doctor's. Either someone had left a visible light burning, or a few leftovers had been unloaded after a raid on Stettin. It was never repeated, but we slept less easily after that.

Chapter Four

BARNIMSKUNOW
Summer 1944 to February 1945
The Russians Are Coming

BY THE SUMMER OF 1944 Germany was facing disaster. On June 4, Rome fell to the Allied forces; on June 6, the Allies landed in Normandy; in July, the Russians crossed into East Prussia.

Gerhart, whose field was international affairs, later wrote that he had foreseen the consequences of the war on Russia and had opposed it, not only on moral grounds but on tactical ones. It was Germany's move against Russia that had led him to cut his ties to the Foreign Office. He spent the years between 1941 and 1944 building a safe haven for Berlin University's library of international affairs. "In the summer of 1944," he wrote, "I realized that defeat was certain. Somehow, the idea of meeting it as a civilian was unbearable to me. So I volunteered for the army. I first served in a divisional radar station at the Eastern front; then I was 'promoted' to front line service."

In September he wrote to Erika: "You have asked me what I do. That is secret and sadly I am not allowed to write it to you. But I can describe to you my uniform, about which you asked. I have a blue-gray cap with a cockade and eagle on it and a blue jacket, which has a white eagle on the right and a brown mirror on the collar. I have blue-gray breeches and a pair of black boots.” He also tells Erika that he shares a room with nine others and asks her to draw or paint a picture of herself, her brother, and mother and send it to him. Gerhart chose to volunteer for the army, but if he hadn't he probably would have been called up. In the fall of 1944 the Germans attempted to replace their losses by drafting an additional half million men, boys between the ages of fifteen and eighteen and men between fifty and sixty years old.

In July came the fateful news of the general retreat of the German army in the East. The Western Front had never seemed real or even important to these Easterners. All their men were on the Eastern Front. The Russians and the Poles were the enemy, the age-long enemy.[7] While Hitler's alliance with Moscow lasted, they had been uneasy. And when he broke it, it seemed to them natural if dangerous. But with the disastrous retreat from Stalingrad in 1943, the greatest disaster that had yet fallen, all their secret and repressed fears of a total German defeat became reality. From then on they knew it was the beginning of the end. Many Pomeranians and a few Barnimskunow boys had been among the troops trapped at Cherkassy.[8] After the losses suffered there,

---

[7] The German resentment of Poland was particularly intense. The Treaty of Versailles, in giving Poland a piece of land with access to the sea and the port of Danzig, had cut East Prussia off from the rest of Germany. Angry at having Poland flung down in the middle of its territory, Germans ignored the fact that the land had originally belonged to Poland. It had been swallowed by Prussia at the end of the 18th century when Poland had been stripped of its sovereignty and divided between the neighboring states of Prussia, Russia and Austria.

[8] German troops were encircled at Cherkassy from mid-December 1943, to February 16, 1944, a final draining away of German offensive strength in the Ukraine. After suffering high casualties, the troops were finally able to break out of the circle but left behind most of their equipment.

the heart had gone out of the villagers. With the news that the Russians had thrust into Romania in the south, entered Poland in the north and were at the borders of East Prussia, life became even grimmer.

One morning, I saw everyone out on the street talking in low tones. Only Herr Schultz, the schoolmaster, was absent. Rumors, terrible rumors, spread; that night the ghastly news was confirmed officially by Goebbels. A desperate band of officers had attempted a *Putsch* to kill Hitler and some of his henchmen, but, though well organized, it failed. Now these courageous men were to be punished as traitors. It struck home to Pomerania. One of the main instigators was a young *Graf* whom everyone knew and whose large estate was not far from us. The affair grew more ghastly, for his wife and children were killed too—the whole family wiped out. Many people who had hitherto been on the fence politically swung abruptly over to the rebel side.[9]

Despite—or perhaps because of—the fear of what would happen if Russian troops crossed into West Prussia, sometime in August 1944 Frau Hecker decided that we must all make an *Ausflug*, a holiday excursion! It was a very comic expedition, involving the most tremendous effort and organization for one day. We were to go to Kolberg, a proud Hansa town northeast of us on the Baltic and a beautiful

---

[9] The conspirators, whose previous attempts to assassinate Hitler had been blocked by the Fuhrer's frequent change of plans, had finally managed to place a bomb in Hitler's conference room. The bomb, hidden inside a briefcase, lay about six feet from Hitler's legs. When the Colonel who had placed the bomb left the room to take a fake phone call, another officer moved into his place, found the Colonel's briefcase in his way, and shoved it to one side. The bomb was now on the far side of a heavy oak plank that supported one end of the conference table. When it exploded, it killed four officers, severely injured several others, and left Hitler shaken but alive.

resort with a long, wide beach and dunes. It was some miles away.

We were awakened about 4 a.m. and sleepily tumbled into the closed carriage awaiting us in the dark *Hof*. There were five children, three adults, and a young Ukrainian boy to drive us. We drove the long way to Stargard in the darkness, to the railroad station, and got our train to the north. It was only then that I noticed Frau Hecker's festive appearance. She was a large woman, though not badly proportioned, but she had decked herself out in an outmoded, red and white striped, billowing summer dress with a tremendous floppy straw hat tied with ribbons under her chin. The two girls were in their best, too. The train was crowded as usual and jolted along, stopping at every little station. But we were all in a holiday mood by now, the children wildly excited. We reached Kolberg about nine or ten o'clock. It was a hot summer's day, but the breeze from the sea was cool, and the Baltic was a brilliant blue. We were in a new, fresh world. I dashed around and saw some of the beauties of the town, and then we had our picnic lunch—very lavish and carefully wrapped—on the dunes. Herr Hecker even bought beer for the three of us. He and the children went bathing in spare underwear, but Frau Hecker and I had to be content with wading, for neither of us had bathing suits.

We tore ourselves away in the middle of the afternoon to get the train. What a ride! Everyone on the train was tired and very hot. Frau Hecker and I got seats at last, the children taking turns sitting in our laps and standing. Vevey and Erika climbed into the baggage nets and curled precariously over our heads, swaying and bumping. The red and white dress was mussed and wrinkled, the hat comically askew, and the children dirty in the immemorial fashion of summer jaunts. It was very late when we reached Stargard. We drove back in the dark to Barnimskunow, the children all asleep, arriving long after midnight. Strenuous as it was, it had been worth the effort. I always liked the Heckers better after our *Ausflug*.

It was also in August that Karl Wegener, Else's eldest son and her darling, came home on a brief leave. He had just received his commission as a lieutenant and had on his brave new uniform. He was a gay, attractive boy, devoted to his mother, and was also a favorite with Frau Schwarz. He healed the breach between the two. During those few days I several times had a bottle of wine with the Wegeners in their garden. Else was so happy, Eva looked her prettiest, and Ernst and Erika and Jerry were all admiration for Karl's gaiety and spirits. He was on his way to the Balkans to defend the oil fields. I had one of the last messages that anyone ever had from him, a postcard he wrote me from a troop train going through Rumania. It was dated August 24, 1944. He was never even reported missing; he just disappeared. The family tried but failed to locate a comrade who had known him, someone who might be able to tell them what had happened. Else hoped for many years that one day she might hear definitely that he had been killed. She was afraid he must be a Russian prisoner, but no fragment of a clue ever came through.

Early in the fall, while our world was breaking up, Else and I had one real outing. About ten miles to the southeast lived a prosperous farmer's family on a big farm. The Marquarts and the Durres had long been friends, but since the war, horses couldn't be spared for just visiting, so they hadn't seen each other for about a year. I think Else and Frau Marquart both realized it might be the last meeting for a long while. They had begged her to come for the afternoon and supper, and she asked to bring me along. She commandeered the surrey and horse and the old Polish driver who had been with them for years, and we drove off with a flourish, two ladies going to make a visit, dressed in our best. It was a lovely, peaceful drive and had the charm of novelty for me. We drove through a more rolling country, and I thought I got a whiff of sea air. But the sky was the same, wide and low, and the tree-lined road as straight as ever. The Marquarts' house was old and square and comfortable, and they were a friendly, hospitable family with that North German dignity I liked. There were only daughters at home, but they were all attractive girls.

We had a lovely time, first coffee and cake and later an excellent farm supper. As the war news was so bad—they had not heard from their sons for too long now—the cheerful atmosphere grew a little sad and muted after supper. Else took an affectionate leave, and we started home about nine o'clock with not a light over the whole wide countryside or over the whole wide world it seemed. We had a carriage lantern, blinded for the blackout, which barely helped us to see the edge of the road.

After a mile or so a sudden storm came up, first wind that blew out our lantern, then lightning, thunder, and wild rain. We put up the carriage curtains, which helped some. Suddenly the surrey lurched, and we were off the high curb into the ditch, but not overturned. The horse and the old man were unnerved, so Else drove. Halfway home the storm cleared, and shortly after we felt the earth tremble under us. Far away on the northern horizon a sudden bright illumination grew, diminished, and spread again. A bombing, where exactly we didn't know. We were glad to get home at last.

Another refugee family had come to stay with the Heckers during the summer. Frau Peltsch, who arrived with her seven-year-old son, was from Aschersleben, a small industrial city in central Germany with many plants manufacturing airplanes. These had been constantly bombed and rebuilt, and Frau Peltsch, whose husband was in the *Luftwaffe*, had been employed in one until it had been wiped out. Living under such conditions had left her nervous and overwrought. Her son, Dieter, was older than Jerry and a nice child, but he, too, was nervous. They brought with them a disturbing breath of city war misery, as well as news of the Western Front, which had been remote from our Eastern country life. Frau Peltsch felt ill at ease and lonely from the first. She despised Barnimskunow and its "primitive," ill-informed inhabitants, particularly the Heckers, who disliked her in turn. She made no friends by accusing the agricultural northeast of not doing its share to aid the war effort, and she was also an ardent National-Socialist, not appreciated in Pomerania, where most people were not.

Whenever she heard from her husband, she was gay and sang for several days, amused the children, and made Erika dolls' clothes out of scraps. She was an excellent seamstress. She made herself a really smart, good-looking coat out of some material she had saved up. When I admired it, she made Erika one out of a very old coat of my husband's, with a hood lined with a piece of red plaid skirt. She also made Jerry a beautiful suit out of some old grey *Luftwaffe* pants of her husband's, shorts and a little jacket. He was very proud of it, and we have it still, as well as Erika's coat. When we had a modest celebration to mark Jerry's sixth birthday on October 31 with a small cake baked by Else and some apples from Frau Hecker, Frau Peltsch presented him with a matching cap that she'd made from an old Luftwaffe tunic.

As the fruits and berries ripened, quite a lot came my way—pears, plums, currants, but mostly apples, "fall" apples from Frau Hecker, Frau Wegener, and one or two friendly cottagers. I dried them all in the sun very carefully and then stored them in bags.

Every day great fleets of American bombers flew high over us. We all knew they were Americans, as the British were known to make only night raids. I had thwarted Jerry in some nefarious enterprise, and to strike back he sputtered the worst thing he could think of: "*Du alt Amerikanische Mutter, Du!*" (You bad old American mother!)

Sometime in that uneasy fall, an epidemic of diphtheria struck our neighborhood, hitting the very elderly the hardest. Dr. Marseilles, the only physician for miles around, drove his old horse and buggy day and night, but his supply of remedies was inadequate. It was sad to see desperately ill old ladies, fully dressed and sitting bolt upright in an old carriage, driving miles to Stargard to the only hospital, most of them to die there.

After the decisive defeats in the East, and especially after the abortive *Putsch*, the gentry became silent and stony-faced. There were no more Sunday suppers. Herr Schultz, as Nazi representative in Barnimskunow, kept to himself, though the villagers were afraid not to be civil to him.

Since living at the Heckers', I no longer went to Stargard weekly for vegetables. Frau Hecker gave me a regular allotment from her garden, and Else supplemented it with what she could. So it was on one of our visits to Frau Stohr in late September that we discovered something new was happening; German refugees were fleeing from East Prussia before the Russians. We saw whole trains of farm wagons driven by women or young boys, loaded with women and children, bedding, food, grain, hay, baby carriages, bicycles, with pots and pans dangling below the wagons. Driving some of the wagons were fur-coated, well-dressed women, and leading one of the lines, was a smart trap with a tweedy young woman at the reins. They all wore high, polished riding boots.

As they plodded slowly past us, heading west in a wavering line, all the Stargarders stared at them, It seemed so fantastic. They stared back, unsmiling, grim, and one country woman called out from her wagon: "It'll be your turn next." They had already been days and even weeks on their slow way. We went home sobered and full of unrest, but even then it didn't seem real. We all knew there was a big Russian offensive in the East, but we hadn't realized they were actually on the march into Germany.

On the last trip we made to Stargard, not only did we see an unbroken line of these nightmarish treks—now they were coming from West Prussia too—but a freight-carload of Italian soldiers, going back to Italy we were told. The crowd was hostile and silent, though the Italians laughed and joked uneasily among themselves.

Cold weather came early that year, and trek after trek clattered down our street, coming slowly out of the East and making for the West to the Oder River. There were few smart vehicles now. Those had long since overtaken the endless line of slow wagons. These were of all sorts, from good solid wagons with big, light-weight balloon tires and strong sleek farm horses driven by women with handsome long fur coats and hats, down to rickety carts with old nags.

When a wagon broke down or a horse gave out, the whole line stopped on the crowded road. Then our village gave them soup and bread and helped with repairs. There was usually at least one bicycle per trek for a boy to scout ahead to find a place to camp for the night or to reconnoiter for the right road and direction. The wagons were topped with a framework covered with canvas or rugs, sometimes handsome Oriental rugs. Some of the treks were long, fourteen or fifteen wagons. Each separate trek represented an entire village. The Government had planned and hoped to carry through an orderly exodus, and this worked during the first months. The orders were that as soon as a village was known to be in the immediate path of the Russians, it was to be ready to leave for the West as soon as the German army had come to take over the livestock. The more eastern villages were to go first; the others progressively to fall in line. This worked in a surprising number of cases, but sometimes the Russians got there first, and like all victorious armies everywhere and in every age, wrought havoc and desolation.

These first Russian troops, drunk with victory (and *Schnaps*) were largely made up of rough Mongolians from the steppes and plains of the Far East, and in that first orgy their officers could not or would not control them. In November, more and more single wagons wandered forlornly through, families who had escaped at the last minute, or after the Germans had recaptured their village. The tales of rape were bad enough—any female between eight and sixty—and I still have no reason to believe they were exaggerated, as I saw evidence.

But the common story of children being taken from their mothers sent a chill through all of us. All boys and girls from eight upward were generally taken and sent somewhere to work in the fields. Often, we were told by these escapees in the wagons, the Russians were kind to the little children and played with them, but with plentiful liquor anything could happen. The one characteristic of the Russians that everyone spoke of was their unpredictability. Any sudden whim could change a Russian from sentimental to brutish and as quickly change him back. Senseless arson, the burning of barns sheltering livestock, livestock they themselves could have used to great advantage, was common.

The sight of these daily treks was no longer just a bad dream to us. It was grim reality. But East Prussia still seemed a far way East, and the German army was still maintaining an Eastern Front. By November the whole *Wehrmacht* (army) seemed to be flowing east from the west and south. An endless stream of trucks, tanks and artillery, manned by white-clad soldiers in their winter uniforms, clanked rapidly over the roads, while the thin unbroken line of treks toiled westward. (The noun "trek" seemed to be used loosely to mean both the train of wagons and the march itself.)

Peenemunde, a very secret and strategic missile experiment station on the Peena Delta north of Stettin, was now completely wiped out, and Stettin had been under severe bombing for months. Three families from there had fled to Barnimskunow. They were the wives and children of the three doctors left for the civilian population of that city. One of the physicians, Dr. Lange, came down for a two-day rest and spent it treating all our children. He was a very kind man and a famous pediatrician in Germany.

By November we were all tense and restless, even the children. School struggled on for another two weeks but abruptly ended when Herr Schultz, along with all the other older men, was called up as a defense corps. The war news from the Western Front became suddenly as real and important, almost, as from the East. Even the most optimistic at last realized that the Germans couldn't hold out much longer. I made no secret of my relief. I think that was also the secret relief of everyone. But in the meantime, our personal plight was becoming desperate. The Russians were on the move in earnest, pushing their forces nearer every day, and it seemed that nothing could stop them now.

Many of us wanted to leave. But how? And where? I knew absolutely no one west of the Oder River in all Germany. My parents-in-law were old and ill in Silesia, as near the Russians as we were. My husband and two brothers-in-law were all on the Eastern Front, one of their wives in Silesia and the other in Berlin.

A young American friend in Berlin, the wife of a German in the army, had written to me earlier that she had gone to Mecklenburg with her two little children to an estate belonging to a Count, whose wife was an American. I had already written to her after seeing our first trek, asking her to find us refuge there. She had kindly but firmly discouraged me. She herself would be very glad to have us, though they were full up with relatives and other refugees, but the Countess (from Boston) told her that another American would be unwelcome. It was too dangerous for her. Her husband was at the front, she was running the huge estate single-handed and, as an American, she was suspect herself.

An Australian friend, also the wife of a German on the front, left Berlin before I did for a village on the German edge of the Bodensee (Lake Constance). She, too, discouraged me—absolutely not a corner available, it was choked with refugees and had been for several years. She did say, however, that if I did decide to come she would be glad to help me in any way she could. I looked on the map: the Bodensee was in the extreme southwest corner of Germany, and as inaccessible now as Timbuctoo. Train transportation was so crippled that I doubted whether we could get there in six months, and we would be under constant bombing.

News that the Allies had been defeated in the West in The Battle of the Bulge and that the Germans had taken the offensive led to a brief wave of optimism among the villagers. The holidays were approaching, and everyone concentrated on giving the children a bit of Christmas spirit. The church was swept and aired by Frau Schwarz and the boys, and we all went in for a silent, candlelit service on Christmas Eve. Frau Hecker gave us a chicken, and we had baked apples for dessert. Later Else asked us over for roast hare, red cabbage, and a bottle of wine.

New Year's with its news of an Allied victory put an end to the villagers' hopes. Everyone felt that 1945 was to be a fateful year.

Like people everywhere, the natives of Barnimskunow were loath to leave their homes unless absolutely forced. Most of them had lived there for many generations, and to the cottagers all Germany west of the Oder, except for Vorpommern, was strange and unknown territory, almost a foreign land. I was surprised how few, even among the gentry, had relatives or friends in the West. Nevertheless, due partly to the Government, but mostly to the more realistic among the villagers, preparations to move were underway. As in Warnitz, Waitendorf, and the other villages, the old men and boys were busy repairing wagons, and the blacksmith's forge was ringing all day.

It was bitter cold now. The few treks that came trickling through were almost the last from East Prussia. The women and children in them were half-frozen in spite of their warm clothes and down quilts. Indeed one baby, who was ill, had frozen to death. In a few days a new string of treks appeared, much more sinister for us since these were Pomeranians from towns and villages that even I had heard of. One day two old wagons full of French P.O.W.s came rattling down the street. They waved and shouted "*Sauve qui peut!*" as they passed, going west to France. Their warning to "Run for your life!" did nothing for our peace of mind. I learned later that all the French were told to do as they pleased, stay and be liberated by the Russians, or go west. Evidently most of them left, for we saw many later, on foot and in wagons that they had probably gotten by trading coffee and cigarettes. Cigarettes had taken the place of money. No one smoked them any more, but a single fag would change hands perhaps ten times and would fetch anything from two cakes of soap to a set of long underpants! Some Frenchmen, but not many, even went to German treks.

I had decided to go with our trek. If we had been in the West, I would have stayed where I was to be "taken" by the Allies. But we were hundreds of miles from any American or British troops, and I was not going to be caught by the Russians if I could help it. I might flourish my American passport and shout in English, but most of those first waves of Russians had never seen a passport, couldn't read even Russian, and didn't know English from German. The local train between Stargard and Pyritz had long ceased to run from lack of fuel, and I had no pull nor any means (cigarettes) to hire a private conveyance. Indeed, there was none available. Horses and vehicles were worth more than their weight twice over in gold, or in coffee or cigarettes. Also, even if I could have gotten to Stettin and there found a train, I was frankly afraid to travel alone as an American with my poor German.

Frau Schwarz and I met one day on the street toward the end of January, and our common bond of fear and anxiety ended our feud: no apologies, of course, we just began talking. She was wildly excited and said she was determined to wait no longer. She didn't know how, but she and a Frau Lange from Stettin, with whom she had become great friends, were going to find a way.

Most of our village wagons were finished and ready by the last week in January, but we had been forbidden to leave by the authorities until they gave the signal. That they wouldn't do until the roads were cleared of the treks from farther east and of the German army still pouring west. We had to wait until a German military unit took over Barnimskunow to protect and use the livestock and open up a field station. The only reason that seemed valid to us all was that we couldn't get out onto the crowded road, anyway, until the last wave of East Prussians and East Pomeranians had passed. It was a physical impossibility.

It was settled that I was to go in the Heckers' family wagon with them. I had had several long conversations with Else, and she was chagrined that she couldn't take us in the Durre wagon. But it was a small one, and there were her sister, her invalid brother, Eva and Ernst, and her husband's aged aunt. It was impossible. She pointed out that the Heckers' wagon was big and sturdy with balloon tires and two strong horses. It was interesting to me that in most of these Eastern villages, the lord of the manor and family, or his wife if he were in the army, elected to wait and go with their villages, instead of dashing off early in a swift vehicle to safety. There was still a sense of noblesse oblige. Even the *Inspektors* could have fled, but none did so far as I know.

Herr Michels, our landowner, was one of the few who

abandoned his village. He and his wife left secretly the day before our trek, their excuse being one of age. It was an unforgivably traitorous act, and no one from Barnimskunow ever forgave or forgot.

That last week only the most necessary work was done, milking the cows and feeding the stock. We were now under Russian artillery fire intermittently day and night. The Russians were ravaging and burning towns and villages twenty miles to the east of us. Treks from East Prussia straggled through, trying to get food or a place to rest their horses, or a place to bury their dead. They had been crowded off the roads by swifter treks or military trucks.

On February 2 we heard that Russian tanks were cutting us off from the Oder, coming up the east bank from the south. The next day Pyritz was in flames from Russian artillery fire. That did it. Pyritz was only fourteen kilometers (about eight miles) south of us. Word went round that night that we were leaving at dawn on February 4, regardless of whether a *Wehrmacht* unit came.

Hurrying home from Else's that afternoon of February 2, I saw a woman, followed by two boys, turning into our *Hof* gate. Her tall, distinguished figure was clad in a long nutria coat, and her straight back was bent under the weight of an out-sized rucksack and two heavy suitcases. That evening, as I came from my room after putting the children to bed, I met her in the corridor, invited her into my warm kitchen, and she told me her story.

She was from East Prussia and a big estate called Caymen, not too far from Konigsberg. Her husband was a landowner, serving as a Lieutenant Colonel on the Eastern Front. After organizing their trek, she had left her mother and mother-in-law, as they had refused to leave their villagers, and, like all older people, dreaded leaving their homes almost more than they dreaded the Russians. She had left to keep the promise she'd made to her husband to get the boys out before the Russians overtook them. Herr Hecker had been a friend of her cousin's, and this was the only address she knew for a stopover west of Konigsberg. To Dorothea Lilienthal,[10] Pomerania still seemed a Western province, but of course she realized now that it was on the wrong side of the Oder. She said they had had a wild trip, mostly by the last trains out from Konigsberg, and were weary and discouraged by what they found here: roads choked up from Konigsberg to Hamburg. The Heckers were not overjoyed to see her, as it meant that three more people would be added to our wagon.

The next morning, February 3, we stood together by the gate to the *Hof*, which was bustling with activity: last-minute details attended to on the wagons, stock milling round, and children dashing in and out. While we stood there, two great waves of silvery planes swept over us, high and aloof, seeming even more remote than usual. For here on the ground the artillery fire was getting louder and nearer all the time. We had another day to wait before we left. Would we get out before we, too, were in flames?

Later Dorothea and I went on a quiet tour of the village. The usual winter scene would have been a ponderous ox hauling a sledge of steaming manure up the long street through mud or over thin ice, or some geese gabbling half-

---

[10] In the manuscript, soon after she meets Dorothea Lilienthal, Mary Jentsch begins to refer to her as Dora. Under ordinary circumstances, German formality would have had them addressing each other as Frau Jentsch and Frau Lilienthal for their entire lifetimes. The urgency and intimacy of their dangerous journey broke down a social structure that had long limited the use of first names to members of the family or close friends of the same social class.

heartedly at the children sliding on the pond, or perhaps a
cat slinking silently along the walls. Now a constant stream
of artillery and trucks rumbled over the ruts, careening
around our corner with soldiers in their white winter garb.
One shouted to us, "*Seid ihr alle verrückt?* (Are you all crazy?) For God's sake get out—the Russky *Panzers* are only
ten kilometers away!"

The geese had vanished overnight, plucked and hanging for the flight. And all the shouting children had been
forced indoors, for two boys had been killed by cruising
Russian scout planes. We met Frau Schwarz, who told us
that residents of Pyritz were fleeing up the railroad track
toward Stargard.

Later that same afternoon I went over to Else's. We
drank a little glass of *Schnaps* and talked quietly for a few
minutes. She insisted on giving me a bottle of wine, several
hard sausages, cheese, the butter she had made yesterday,
and two hundred marks (I had only about seven hundred
in my purse).

Best of all she had already procured for me the used,
but still good, farmer's high boots for which she had traded God knows what. They were three sizes too large but,
strange to say, with two pairs of wool socks in them they
never chafed and were the most comfortable shoes I ever
had. I still have them. We felt far from cheerful, though we
told each other we'd be in the same trek and could "visit"
whenever we wanted. (Their wagon was only a so-called
ladder wagon and already carefully packed with straw, hay,
food, and clothing, down bedding, and a few kitchen utensils.) The trek would stick together, and she and I both knew
that we would be in the same fleet, but each of us also knew
we would be in separate boats.

* * * * * *

That noon the military did come to take over. They took
the stock and began turning Frau Wegener's house into a
Lazaret (field station). We were especially glad to see them,
since for the last two nights the Polish workers had been
on the rampage. The *Commandant* of the regiment had already released them, as there was no question now of saving Barnimskunow. They were told to stay or leave, as they
wished, but no more food was given out, no vehicles provided for them, and there was no authority left to control
them. They had looted several cottages during an artillery
bombardment. Most of the Ukrainians left on foot. Most
of the Poles stayed, but a few of each who wanted to leave,
those most trusted by the Germans they worked for, were
taken on some of the wagons to drive or help out.

I had already done most of my packing. Frau Hecker had
told me I could take two suitcases and our bedding (I had
acquired two feather beds), and, of course, our three rucksacks with our old travel rugs rolled up on the outside. I had
an old army blanket, Erika had a light travel rug a friend
had presented me with when we left Geneva, and Jerry was
allotted my small Chilean rug made of natural brown, black,
and white, plaid llama wool, a prized possession. We were
embarking on a journey of unknown destination and duration, and I knew that whatever was left behind could never
be replaced. But I was sure of one thing: I would not load
myself and the children with more than we could carry on
our backs, our necks, and in our hands.

This was my guide throughout my packing, and I was
ruthless. One suitcase, the smaller, had to be filled with

food. I discarded my good strong suitcases and selected two large flimsy cardboard ones as being lighter. Automatically, I flung aside some of our newer but lighter clothes, and packed only the warmest of our winter things. Summer, if it ever came again, would have to take care of itself. In each rucksack I put in the inevitable felt *Pantoffels* (slippers), two changes of warm underwear, one nightgown apiece, and our only extra shoes. I had a pair of low-heeled brown oxfords, and the children each a pair of scuffed and mended ones. In Jerry's little rucksack (he was just past six) I put all the stockings and socks we possessed. They were the most important single item and had the advantage of being light.

Now for my silver and linen, which Mutter had sent me from Silesia a few months before. This was hard, but silver is heavy. I selected six old silver teaspoons, four silver serving spoons, a knife and fork apiece, a kitchen knife, and a saucepan. With scarcely a backward glance I stuffed the rest into a suitcase with all my best linen and shoved it under a bed without even bothering to look for the key to lock it. What did it matter? Either the Russian bombs would destroy it, or the Poles would loot it first (I hoped the latter). In any case I would never see it again, and of course I never did.

It cost me a pang, however, to leave behind my favorite possessions: a piece of old silver given me by the editor I worked for at Houghton Mifflin all those years ago in Boston and some of my grandmother's big spoons. From my linen I selected one bath towel, three hand towels, and one dish towel. It didn't take me long to sort out my jewels. What little I had would not overburden us. Next I sorted out valuable papers, passports, birth certificates, and the children's birth registrations at the American consulate in Geneva, which proved them to be Americans. These I stuck into my leather briefcase along with a few family photographs. I burned up all my old letters and left behind all the little treasures that I valued for their beauty or their sentiment. One plate, three bowls, and three enameled mugs I packed in the food suitcase. You can eat meat from a bowl but not soup from a plate.

Now came the question of books. I had taken a few of our favorites with us from Berlin when I was last there. My hand naturally gravitated to my little old red leather Nelson edition of Jane Austen in five slim volumes. Not only had they been my never-failing companions for about twenty-five years, but they had a special sentimental value: They had been given me on my fifteenth birthday by my dear old Katy, who couldn't read or write. (She always gave me books, at my carefully written request.) I felt I shouldn't take them all, but which to choose: *Emma*, *Persuasion*, or *Pride and Prejudice*? I put them all aside. This was my only major mistake. I should have taken them all. They were really very light. Then I consulted Jerry and Erika. We could take just one book, but it must be one that we all three liked. This was most difficult. We finally chose Rudyard Kipling's *The Jungle Book*. It was a happy choice, but it was years before I could read it again. We read it at least sixty times in the course of the next year, and each one of us knew the first word on each page before it was turned.

After a hasty midday meal of stew on February 3, I found Frau Hecker coming out of the storeroom, locking the door behind her. She gave me three big sausages, *Dauerwursts* that would keep forever, a jar of fat, flour, and meal. She packed for the trip sides of bacon and ham and everything else she could squeeze in, but later on the trek I found she was the scandal of the villagers, who were bitterly outraged. She had committed a piece of unbelievable folly, due to her miserliness, but mostly due to her stupidity. Instead of handing out everything she couldn't take with her to the villagers, she left it all in the storerooms and locked them! Dora and I could hardly believe our ears, and even Else didn't think she could be such a fool.

That night I carefully packed our food suitcase. The sausages, fat, margarine, sugar, meal, flour, salt, a little jar of jam and a package of *Kunsthonig*,[11] and the light bags of fruits I had dried in the fall. I put a small bag of these in each child's rucksack. Also, I took a big piece of cheese and two loaves of bread. This coarse dark German war bread kept edible for days, and I am convinced it was one of the factors that kept us healthy.

After I had put the children to bed for the last time—the last time we were to sleep in beds for weeks—I went into the living room. There I found Frau Hecker and Frau Lilienthal and Tante and Onkel. Herr Hecker had just come in from the *Hof,* dirty and disheveled, and was opening a bottle of very old currant wine. Frau Hecker was disheveled, too, and distraught. I felt really sorry for them. They were leaving all their possessions, their home and their life here, as were all the Barnimskunowans.

Dora and I felt detached. She had already made her great break with the past, and I had made so many in the last nineteen years that I was only dreading the inscrutable future. She and I could hardly wait to leave this doomed village, no matter what the unknown held for us. But later I was to remember with affection and nostalgia those eighteen peaceful months of security under the big sky of Pomerania, and

[11] Artificial honey, which, given the prevalence of the crop, was probably made of beet sugar.

above all, Else Wegener's friendship and generosity.

The Heckers had been trying for days to convince their two old people that they must go on the trek with us. They were both determined to stay. Old and frail, they hadn't the heart to face the certain hardships and uncertain future. They hadn't long to live anyway, so why be a burden to everyone, including themselves? This was all too true, but we would all have felt badly leaving them behind. Many old people felt this way, and some of the old cottagers did stay. I have never found out what became of them. Finally after more cajoling and threatening on the part of their nephew, the elder Heckers reluctantly gave their consent.

Dorothea and I said good night and walked slowly down the corridor. There was bright moonlight outside, and work in the *Hof* was still going on. The idea of this winter flight, at a nightmarishly slow pace, with terror at our back and perhaps starvation or worse before us, suddenly struck us with full force. Tired and discouraged as we were, it might be easier to be crushed out by the artillery in our beds tonight. The sound of the long-range artillery fire, a dull, heavy, thudding noise, was strange and new, but it didn't strike terror into me as did the sound of sirens and bombing. I went to bed with the windows rattling and the house shaking. I didn't know just where the guns were, how far away, and it didn't seem to matter much.

There is a German version of the children's rhyme:
Ladybird, ladybird fly away home
Your house is on fire, your children will burn.

I used to hear the children chanting it in the spring all over Germany and it goes like this:

Maikäfer flieg!
Der Vater ist in Krieg
Die Mutter ist in Pommerland
Pommerland ist abgebrannt
Maikäfer flieg!

May-beetle fly!
Your father's in the war
Your mother is in Pommern-land
Pommern-land is all in flames
May-beetle fly!

I learned that the rhyme dated from the Thirty Years War, when Pommern was devastated by the armies of Tilly, Wallenstein, and Gustavus of Sweden, and *"Pommerland ist abgebrannt"*—Pommerland is all in flames—became a sinister prediction that I couldn't get out of my mind.

Chapter Five

FLIGHT
February to April 1945
"Pommerland ist abgebrannt"

IN THE WINTER OF 1945, Mary received news that Gerhart was fighting in Cosel in Upper Silesia. That same month the Russians invaded East Prussia. When months passed with no further word, she had to accept the fact that he had either been killed or taken prisoner by the Russians.

By February, with the Russian troops advancing, the Barnimskunow Trek set out to the relative safety of the western shore of the Oder River, which after the war would become a boundary between Germany and Poland. An estimated twelve to fourteen million Germans who had lived for generations in Silesia, Pomerania, Prussia, and other areas that would become post-war Poland made an exodus. It is believed that as many as two million Germans died on treks westward. Many of those who survived lived in temporary shelters for years after the war.

On February 4—a day that dawned overcast with a bleak wind—we were all awakened at four o'clock. I dressed Erika in warm underwear, one pair of cotton and one pair of wool stockings, a pair of wool socks, wool slip, a pleated wool skirt and sweater, a pair of cotton-knit "training *Ho-*

sen" (a sort of seat pants that all the German children wore during the war), her new coat with hood, and my old ski boots from Geneva. She had mittens in her pocket and a red toboggan cap. I wanted to protect her from the cold, but I also wanted to make more room in the luggage.

Jerry had warm underwear, a wool knit sweater and shorts, his *Luftwaffe* suit, and Erika's old, outgrown, one-piece snowsuit with zipper, a knitted cap over his ears, and Erika's old ski boots. Despite their layers of clothing, the children were jumping up and down in excited anticipation of the Great Adventure.

I put on two pairs of cotton stockings, three pairs of wool socks, a thin wool skirt, a silk blouse, and my one and only thin wool dress. It was quite elegant when I managed to get it in Berlin in 1942. On top of that I wore an old, thin, black pony skin coat I had bought in Geneva, and my heavy clumsy new coat made in the village. Then I pulled on my great boots. We looked—and what was worse, felt—exactly like sausages, but I had to save space in the suitcases for underwear, two dresses for Erika, extra pants and shirts for Jerry, a wool skirt and two more blouses for me. We each had a toilet kit and an extra sweater in the rucksack.

Jerry was convinced that his tricycle would be useful for scouting, and for Berlin and New York when we got there. He was sure we would go through Berlin on the way to America, and he could have one ride around Innsbrücker Platz. I had to tell them they could each take a couple of small toys as long they fit in their pockets. Jerry took a little hammer, and later I found his pockets stuffed with nails, screws, and bits of wire. The hammer proved useful.

Erika's most beloved toy was a foot-high, stuffed koala bear given her in Geneva by an Australian friend of mine,

Maisie Grieg. She took White Ear to bed every night. It never occurred to her that he was too big to take with us. But he was not only big, but too hard. Couldn't he stick his head and arms out of her rucksack so as not to take up so much room? I finally persuaded her that it was impossible, that she needed that space for her extra shoes. She cried a little but at the last minute tucked him into her bed, kissed him, and covered him gently. This was my worst moment. She stuck a small doll and a couple of doll's dishes into her pocket and was ready.

I looked around the room for a last time and saw my good warm dressing gown, but it was too bulky, and I hung it on a nail. I shoved three full suitcases under the bed and didn't even lock my trunk with its summer clothes. I did put my name and improbable American address in the suitcase with the silver, though naturally I never saw it again. The last thing I did before leaving the room was to cut a slit in Jerry's snowsuit from the end of the zipper to the end of the crotch and on through his knit pants. There would never be time for him to peel off the snowsuit and fumble through all the layers when he went to the john.

We had a quick but good hot breakfast: hot milk, ersatz coffee, bread and margarine, and *Wurst*. Then we went out to the dark *Hof*. The cows had just been milked, and the men were filling the big milk cans by lantern light to take with us. All the children were beside themselves, running between the horses' legs, clambering over the big wagon wheels, talking to the soldiers, rushing to take a last look at a pet rabbit. Our big wagon stood ready with a thick layer of hay covering the floor. Since the baggage still had to be stored around the edge and covered with bedding for seats, I ran quickly over to Else's. Her house was already functioning as a field hospital with the wounded in the beds, and soldiers were all over the street and the farm. The village already seemed strange and alien in this hour of desertion.

Back at our *Hof* I looked with misgiving at the loaded wagon and the twenty-three people, ranging in age from seven months to eighty-nine years, who had to fit into it. There were twelve children: three Heckers, Frau Günther's two, two little ones belonging to the overseer, Hermann and Ernst Lilienthal, Erika and Jerry, and a seven-month-old baby belonging to one of the two cottage women who had joined us because they had no wagon of their own. In addition to the two cottagers, the adults consisted of a Polish boy, who had elected to go with us as driver; Tante and Onkel Hecker; Frau Hecker; Frau Günther and her mother, Frau Recklies; Dora and I; and the wife of one of the overseers. The two overseers were already gone, called up in the final days of the war, when the country was being scoured for soldiers. One was in the *Wehrmacht* and the elder was with Herr Schultz in the Old Man's Army. Only at this moment did I learn that Herr Hecker had to stay to finish turning over the estate to the *Wehrmacht*. He was to follow later on his bike.

Though most of the people were leaving behind their possessions and the only homes they knew, there was a general feeling of relief. Action at last after the nervous tension of waiting! The cans of fresh milk were put into the trailer cart along with the pig that had been hurriedly slaughtered two days before, and hay for the horses.

At last, the confusion resolved into order. We were all to start out riding in the wagon, with Tante and Onkel safely stowed in the warmest spot. Later, I learned, able-bodied women and children were to walk beside the wagon as much as possible to save the horses. With Frau Hecker's largest rugs nailed to the framework and our feather beds spread over us, the interior was as warm and cozy and smelly as the cow barn, though not as sweet.

Herr Hecker raised his arm in signal, the Polish boy cracked his whip, and we pulled out of the *Hof*. As we turned into the street, the fourteen other wagons fell into place behind us. There was a tremulous moment when we left the village, but out on the high road, headed north, spirits rose, and we began to feel like the hardy adventurers we were. The big farm horses (our wagon had four) were stepping out now and tossing their manes in the chill air. We were on our way!

We journeyed past Warnitz, which was deserted with only soldiers about, across the railroad tracks, and due west toward the Oder. Our nearest bridge over the Oder was only some seventeen kilometers (about ten miles) away, slightly south of us at Griefenhagen, but to our great dismay, some soldiers stopped us and said it was now impossible to reach it. Russian tanks were cutting us off, coming up from the south between us and the Oder. It was our first setback. We turned due north toward Stargard. The sun was high when we got there, and the town was quiet. As we skirted its edge, I thought of that first trek I had seen in Stargard, from East Prussia. It was our turn now.

Later, when I was walking, I watched our whole outfit pass by. A few wagons were covered with rugs, others with patched tarpaulins, others with bedspreads and old comforters, and still others with bits of corrugated iron and tin. All were lined with abundant straw, and cook pots and kettles, baby carriages and baby pots hung from the sides. A slaughtered pig was stretched across the back of one wagon;

they hadn't had time to butcher it. Axes, saws, hatchets, coils of rope, and extra harnesses were tied on where there was room, and there were at least three bicycles. A few geese and chickens squawked rebelliously from within. After months of watching the endless line plodding westward, we had become a part of it.

Our hopeful refrain for weeks had been "Once across the Oder," because it had always been said that the Russians would stop at the Oder. The Oder was our Red Sea. Once across it, we would feel safe. On the further shore lay the promised land of Mecklenburg and Vor-Pommern to the north. Many of our companions intended to leave the trek to stay in various towns there. Even if they knew no one, they thought they'd be safe and near enough to return home as soon as the war had ended. No one has yet returned; Pommern is now Polish. Barnimskunow and the houses and the farm buildings were destroyed.

The Heckers had some relatives near Schwerin, the largest city in Mecklenburg, and they intended to end their trek there. Dora and I were untrammeled by any plans, though I still vaguely thought of my friend Jane in that castle. I had the address. The thing was to cross the Oder, and the rest would take care of itself. Our worst fear was the lack of food in the West. How many hundreds of thousands of Eastern refugees had preceded us, eating their way like a scourge of locusts as they passed?

After leaving Stargard behind, all the able-bodied got out and walked. How good the fresh air seemed after the stuffy, cramped wagon! All was quiet and peaceful: no tanks, no sound of artillery, not even a plane in the sky. I found Else and Eva, and we walked along together for a while. Eva was already regretting abandoning some of her pretty clothes and talked ruefully of the little flask of expensive French perfume. Else told me that Frau Schwarz had actually wangled a small truck and, with Frau Lange, their two families, a great deal of baggage, and some small pieces of furniture, had left Barnimskunow the day before in a cloud of dust and triumph.

We were all quite cheerful and gay, the children skipping along in the warm winter sun. We had only to get to Stettin, now our nearest bridge, and we would make that in a couple of days.

Someone started singing an old tune from the days of horse-drawn carriages, and it became our theme song for the next year with its gay melody and a romantic air:

> *Hoch auf dem gelben Wagen*
> *sitz ich beim Schwager vorn;*
> *vorwarts die Rosse traben,*
> *lustig schmettert das Horn.*
> *Felder, Wiesen, and Auen,*
> *Schaumendes Ahrengold.*

And the refrain:
> *Ich ware so gerne geblieben,*
> *Aber der Wagen der rollt.*

> High on the yellow coach
> I sit in front with the coachman.
> The white horses start trotting,
> Merrily peals the horn.
> Meadows, pastures, and marshes,
> Ripening grain shimmering gold
> How I would like to stay,
> But the coach rolls on.

Before dusk fell, the baker's boy scouted ahead on his bike to find us lodgings for the night. The artillery started up again, though faintly, the air grew chill, and it began to snow. At the third village we were able to find rooms to house the old and the very young and a paddock for the horses. The rest of us spent a cold, wet night trying to sleep in the straw in our wagons, awakened by the artillery fire, which sounded very close. We pulled out at break of day, most of us glad to be trudging along the hard, rutted road, stretching our legs and keeping warm. The horses, breath steaming in the cold air, were holding up well. The noise of the artillery seemed further away, and we had seen no Russian tanks.

Late in the afternoon it began to snow again very lightly. Many of the villagers' boots had been patched and mended until the leather was almost gone and they were scarcely fit to walk in. Some wore wooden clogs. The more fortunate people in the village had distributed clothes and children's outgrown shoes to the needy, but there were no extra shoes and boots for adults. However, everyone was still cheerful. We had breakfasted on warmed milk and cheese, and the children were enjoying themselves. There was laughing and joking and singing as we tramped on in groups of two or three.

Dark of the second day found us in a disorganized village called Seefeld. An hour before we got there we were startled to hear loud artillery fire, an experience that was evidently new to the Seefelders, who were in a panic. About forty of us found shelter in a big farmhouse on the edge of a lake or river, we couldn't see which. The house, already overrun with strangers who had staked out claims in every corner, was ablaze with light, the big kitchen stove was glowing red, and every passerby thrust in a stick of wood or a shovelful of coal, as they heated milk in whatever pot or pan they could find. We never knew who was the farmer's wife or, indeed, if she were even there. Dora and I managed to warm the last of the Barnimskunow milk and gave it to the four children. Then, as there were no more corners available, we put them to bed in the middle of the parlor.

They slept, but we didn't, kept awake by the artillery, which went on all night. We were glad to get off early next morning. It always took us a good hour and a half to get the wagons harnessed up, the people assembled, and the whole trek started off. Dora now took over from the Polish boy. He was no organizer, and Frau Hecker was of even less use, especially as she had heard no word from her husband. With the help of one or two of our capable but rheumatic old men and her oldest boy, Hermann, Dora whipped us into shape. She and nine-year old Ernst took turns driving our wagon from then on.

The next two days were bad. The artillery fire was constant and alarmingly close. The roads became hourly more crowded with earlier treks ahead of us and other newcomers from this area trying to wedge in between. At last we came to a fork bearing slightly west, and to our joy it was comparatively empty except for the army. We had not gone half a mile before some German soldiers stopped us. "Turn off at once." Russian *Panzers* were coming up. "*Aber schnell!*" So we had to strike off across the frozen fields with treacherous icy spots of marsh. Every little while a horse slipped and foundered, or a wheel broke and had to be mended, holding up the whole train for half an hour or so. To be fleeing for one's life at the pace of farm horses was a strain on us all.

At the end of four days we had covered only some thirty miles. There were mutterings from some wagons about leaving the trek, but they were persuaded by some of our more responsible members to stay on. We felt that if we should be caught by the Russians there was safety in numbers. But the troop movements were forcing us northeast instead of west. At times we were even going due east. North of Stettin it would be impossible for our wagons to cross the river, for that's where the great delta of the Oder began. In Barnimskunow there had been some talk of getting on one of the boats taking refugees across the Baltic to the Mecklenburg port of Rostock, or further west to a Holstein port. Dora told us that many boatloads had left Konigsberg, but several had been sunk, and all the women and children drowned in the cold waters of the Ostsee. I would rather take my chances on land.

We were already slightly north and quite a bit east of Stettin. We floundered along trying to force our way southwest. We had no official leader, for Herr Hecker had never turned up. But it made no difference; it was just a question of holding our own in the right direction. At the end of the fifth day (I think it was the fifth) we found ourselves in Muelkenthin (pronounced Milkenteen), about thirty miles from Barnimskunow, a village with a large, ancient castle and an enormous *Hof*. Many refugees were established there, at least three big treks. We scattered for the night, some in the village half a mile down the road and some joining us in the castle. To find a room we had wandered into great halls with beautiful old sixteenth- and seventeenth-century furniture and hangings, all full of people with their bedding spread out on the floors. I never heard the name of the *Herr Graf*, but I saw the *Gräfin*, a calm, elderly woman with an interesting face and pleasant manners. We finally found space in the rabbit warren of little rooms down in the vast vaulted cellar. Together we cooked on the stove in one of the big kitchens, a good hot supper of stew from the last fresh meat and vegetables from Barnimskunow. Then we settled down snugly for the night in our bedding on the floor. It was the first good night, and we felt very safe. The walls of the castle seemed so thick and invulnerable that we paid no heed to the bombing of the artillery, which seemed farther away than usual.

Next morning was bright and cold. Another trek had come in during the night, and little fires were snapping gaily all over the *Hof,* both for warmth and for cooking. There must have been at least five hundred "guests" within the castle walls, not to mention the horses and wagons. Jerry and Erika found the Lilienthals, explored the castle park, and played in the *Hof.* After an early lunch of bread and *Wurst,* I walked to the village alone and found Else, who was established in the house of the miller, a family acquaintance.

The miller's wife offered me a cup of real coffee and delicious fresh bread in her big, cheery kitchen. It was pleasant to put aside for a moment the urgency of our plight, but I was soon recalled to it. The Muelkenthin Trek, they said, had been all ready and scheduled to leave at least four days ago, but they couldn't get out. Their scouts had reported that all roads to the Oder were impassible, not only crowded with treks, but blocked by the many broken-down wagons. And worse, more and more roads and even fields were now cut off by Russian tanks. Some treks had already been overtaken by the tanks. I took hasty leave, waving a casual *Auf Wiedersehen* to Else, though it proved to be farewell.

Back at the castle four young German officers who had come down from the north last night and bivouacked in the *Hof,* were talking to Dora, telling her we had no chance if we stayed on with the trek. The Russians were swarming in from the east, their tanks coming up from the south in a steady stream. They said that if we could be ready in ten minutes they would take us in their truck as far toward Stettin as they could, and perhaps we could get a lift the rest of the way.

Dora and I and the children took up our suitcases, shouldered our rucksacks, and, abandoning our cook pot and warm bedding to the bewildered Frau Recklies, left a message for Frau Hecker, and clambered into the back of the truck. We drove down the village street past the miller's house and onto the *Panzer* road, the only way possible. Our driver maneuvered behind a barn and then dashed down the road on an empty stretch before turning into a little dirt road. It was exhilarating to go bumping along, fast at last in the right direction. They took us farther than they dared.

I have no idea just where they put us down, but it was a big, safe crossroad—free of tanks, they said—and some truck would be sure to pick us up soon. We walked up and down to keep warm for about three-quarters of an hour. As dusk fell, our high spirits sank. Two women in a strange place, in the open, encumbered with baggage, and responsible for four children ranging from twelve to six. Had we been too brash? We were almost run down by a truck before it saw us and stopped. We scrambled in, scarcely waiting for an invitation. These soldiers took us into East Stettin, a big city that seemed very dark and quiet until an unearthly wail engulfed us. I hadn't heard a real city siren since Berlin. The truck dropped us hastily at the railroad station, and, amid what seemed thousands of women and children, we were hustled deep down into a brightly lighted air raid shelter. The vastness of it—the masses of people and the electric lights—bewildered us, country folk as we were. There were benches all along the walls and rows of benches in the middle, nearly all full. We heard the bombs fall and strike somewhere near: first the peculiar whistling shriek streaking through the air and rising to a high scream, before the dull thunder—a series of detonations blending into one another with greater and greater force. Long after the last bomb had struck, the earth still rumbled with the delayed dissolving of brick and mortar into rubble. There were two more strikes that night. I thought of our castle fortress at Muelkenthin, the *Hof* with its little cook-fires, the horses and wagons, and the crowd of "serfs." It seemed medieval now in comparison, unreal, rather like the battle scene in Sir Lawrence Olivier's film of *Henry V.* Even the artillery in retrospect seemed harmless as I dozed on the hard bench in the shelter.

After the end alarm, when the raiders had gone, people went up for air. Dora and Hermann went to find out about trains. No more that night they were told, but she and I went up in turns until daylight, just to be sure. At the end of the first raid, some high-school girls (from the *Bund Deutsche Mädchen*) brought us potato soup, bread, and margarine. We had no trouble keeping the children all together. They didn't want to budge from our bench.

We climbed up very early the next morning to the station platform in time to see more high-school girls, pale and drawn in the bitter cold air, trying to comfort some young mothers whose babies had frozen during the long night. It had been below zero, and they had elected to stay out in the desperate hope of getting a train. Though the babies had been swathed in fur and wool, most of those under a year hadn't sufficient body warmth and vitality to withstand the prolonged cold. It was a sight I hope never to see again: these young girls wresting a score of dead babies from their frantic mothers. "But he was breathing just a minute ago," one cried unbelievingly.

After a hasty breakfast of ersatz coffee and bread, handed out to us by Stettin women, we milled around the platform with thousands of others all that endless morning, stamping to keep warm, jockeying for position near the tracks, one of us always staying by our baggage.

Every person concentrated on getting a train that day. An urgency engulfed us all, our last chance. Two trains appeared and were stormed by the mob; the lucky ones got on, and they pushed off without us. Many times we had got ourselves in a strategic place only to be shoved back by the mob. Dora and I shoved and pushed with the rest. Mother love, I decided, was one of the most selfish forces the human race was heir to. When her children's welfare and lives were at stake, each mother was aroused to an animal singleness of purpose, to protect her young. Dora and I were exactly like the others.

We grew more desperate with every hour. The rumor spread and grew that the last, the absolutely last, train out of Stettin for anywhere, was due from the east around three p.m. How many times we got to the tracks with our baggage only to be pushed back by others or squeezed onto the rails! It was a panicking mob, aggressive and frightening, and we were part of it.

Our four children behaved admirably. Erika and Jerry were two years older now than when they had come to

Pommern. They realized the seriousness of the situation, and the bombing of the night before had frightened them. I had told Erika never to lose sight of me, to hang on to Jerry's hand for dear life. She had already developed a great sense of responsibility, and I knew I could count on her, though she wouldn't be ten for two more days. Jerry, just six, neither complained nor lagged. Thrust by chance together for better or worse, comradeship with the Lilienthals had ripened quickly, and we looked upon ourselves as one family. We felt we had known each other for years.

We were a handsome lot; three of us blond and three dark. The Lilienthals were unusually handsome and attractive, all three with high, Slavic cheekbones and sparkling dark eyes. Hermann, twelve, was a tall, well-made boy, intelligent, sensitive and thoughtful. Ernst-Albrecht, called Lütti ("the little one" in the East Prussian dialect) was compact, sturdy and manly, an extrovert, a mimic and a humorist. He and Erika became special friends. Later, Hermann took a particular interest in Jerry and entertained him by the hour.

About 2:45, the *Fliegeralarm* sounded again. Dora and I looked at each other; yes, we'd risk it and stay on the platform in case the last train came. The station authorities had long given up trying to control the mob, and no one could make us go down in the shelter. We cowered together at our post during the bombing. At least if we were struck, we'd all be killed together. But it finally ended, and twenty minutes later a long, battered train pulled in from the east, groping its way along the rails uncertainly, for children and even a baby in a baby carriage were pushed in front of it by the desperate mob. As was usual now, not a door, not an unbroken window remained.

People surged aboard before it had stopped. Unluckily, we found ourselves opposite a hospital car full of amputees hastily evacuated from Eastern Front hospitals. When we tried to get on, the orderlies kept shouting that this was strictly military, absolutely no civilians allowed. We were desperate. The rest of the train was overflowing, and we no longer had a chance. But Dora doesn't give up easily. She said her husband was a lieutenant colonel and that we six must be taken. While she was talking, she pushed the four children through the windows and was hauled up herself. I handed up the suitcases and rucksacks to her and was pulled aboard myself just as the train pulled slowly off. Other people saw us and flung themselves in, too. The hospital car was now as choked as the others.

As we left the station, I was numb with relief and would have collapsed if there had been any place to collapse to. We rumbled slowly across the long bridge that spans the fateful river and were over the Oder at last. A long, composite sigh of relief passed through the car, like the sound of the wind. Vor-Pommern was separated in our minds from Ost- or Hinter-Pommern by a psychological gulf far wider and deeper than the Oder, a gulf that the Russians could not cross.

Now human decency came back to us all. We became normal, kind, and helpful human beings, trying to sort out the children from the baggage, and the amputees, many in great pain, squeezed together to make one seat more for a tired mother or child. I looked about me. All six of us were scattered through the car. I called to the children and heard them answer but could not see them. We were packed in tightly and though the train was unheated, the crowds soon generated a stuffiness that passed for warmth.

Bundles, boxes, suitcases, rucksacks and go-carts were piled helter-skelter all over the floor, and we humans were wedged among them unable to move. For the next thirteen hours, as long as we were on the train, I stood on one foot, never able to put the other down flat. One arm was clamped and immobilized against my side. In each coat pocket was a sandwich for the children, but I couldn't have taken them out even if Erika and Jerry had been next to me. We rattled and clanged through this corner of Vor Pommern and into the Promised Land of Mecklenburg as dusk came on, but I was scarcely conscious of it. I had no thought of fear now. I was simply preoccupied with my acute personal discomfort. People tried to shift a little, but we couldn't move the baggage. When we stopped at the station of Pasewalk in Vor-Pommern, we all hoped someone would get off. Perhaps they wanted to but couldn't.

As darkness fell and we crawled along at a snail's pace, we spewed a fiery banner through the dark sky, an aerial wake that proclaimed us to all bombers. We were burning coal dust. Dora and I had deliberately drunk no water and only a few swallows of our breakfast coffee in Stettin, but though we tried to ration the children, we were too distraught to supervise them. We both knew by experience that in a train as crowded as this one, the toilets would be inaccessible.

I was soon roused from my numbness by children clamoring for the john. The amputees rapidly solved the problem for the little boys. Many hands passed the boys overhead until they reached the hands of the seated wounded, who held them out the window. The same was done for the tiny girls, though with more difficulty. Jerry was held up twice, just for the fun of it I think. We suddenly pulled to a stop in what seemed to be fields, and to my horror I heard Erika's voice timidly calling to me that she had to "go to the bathroom." She sounded desperate. She was hauled through two compartments to where I stood, and two amputees managed to get to their feet and hold her out the window until she dropped to the ground. I was unable to move or even to speak. Total darkness, Erika alone on the ground: it was a nightmare. What if the train started? It didn't, and somehow the two soldiers managed to catch her hands and pull her back up into the car again.

We continued on all night stopping once or twice at a town, and then again in the fields, and all the while I was standing on one foot. About four-thirty a.m. we stopped at another town and some people got off. They said it was Bad Kleinen, which I later found out is about one hundred twenty-five miles from Stettin. We vaguely knew that it was somewhere in the middle of Mecklenburg, and, as so many got out, Dora and I, shouting to each other across the car, suddenly decided to leave too. I could scarcely get off the train, my leg was so paralyzed with cramp.

Bad Kleinen was the most forlorn and dirtiest station we were ever in. We laid the children out like sardines on a long table, and they were dead to the world for several hours. Dora and I took turns dozing on one chair or lying on the floor. There were several *Fliegeralarms*, and somebody made us go down to the bunker for the first one, but we wouldn't budge for the others. We were too tired. Bad Kleinen was on one of the regular bombing routes to the East, and we sleepily figured that it would be only bad luck if a few were loosed on us on a return trip. Indeed, we found out that all of the Mecklenburg sky was crisscrossed with bombing routes from over the North Sea to Berlin and Stettin.

We now had the proud status of official refugees. This

meant that whatever rides we could wangle—train, truck or wagon—were free. Wherever we stopped on our East-West flight—city, town, or village—as refugees we were entitled to some form of shelter covered with clean straw to sleep on, and two meals a day, breakfast (ersatz coffee, one or two slices of bread with either margarine or *Kunsthonig*) and supper. This was usually a thick potato or cabbage soup, with or without other vegetables, and a slice of bread. This we supplemented with a lunch of *Wurst* and cheese and bread from our food suitcases. Occasionally each child was given a big raw carrot and once even an apple. Our food suitcases held out surprisingly long. I felt very smug about my sacks of dried fruit. It meant a lot to the children, both for health and as a thirst quencher.

There seemed to be only one catch to being a refugee: we had to be always on the move. We were housed and fed three days, but on the fourth we must be off. Only the really ill could remain longer. We were the last wave of hundreds of thousands who had preyed on the meager supplies, and I was amazed that it was all still so well-organized and that we could be fed at all. As refugees, our food cards were theoretically still valid, but actually we could only buy bread on them. Whenever we entered a town by train, truck, or foot, we always found women and schoolgirls to lead us to the hay. In villages, it was always in a schoolhouse; in towns, a schoolhouse or movie theatre; and in cities, either of these or a hall of some kind. As a rule, the hay was thick and changed every day, but sometimes there was either no time between groups of us, or there was no fresh supply.

After the children had waked and we had been given our breakfast, we wandered outside the station a while and then decided to try for a train west to Schwerin, the largest

Mary Hunt as a child
in Louisville, Kentucky

1921: Gerhart writes jokingly to
Mary on the reverse of his photo,
"I hope that everyone in America
is not like you, so that one day I
will be able to accept the invitation
to return."

Mary Hunt in the 1920's

Hedwig and Erdman Jentsch

1940: Erika and friend in Langenbielau

A panoramic view of Langenbielau

1942: Erica and Jerry start school in Langenbielau.

Erica wears a *Tornister* to carry her lunch and books.

1942: Jerry and Erika back in Berlin in Schöneberg Stadtspark

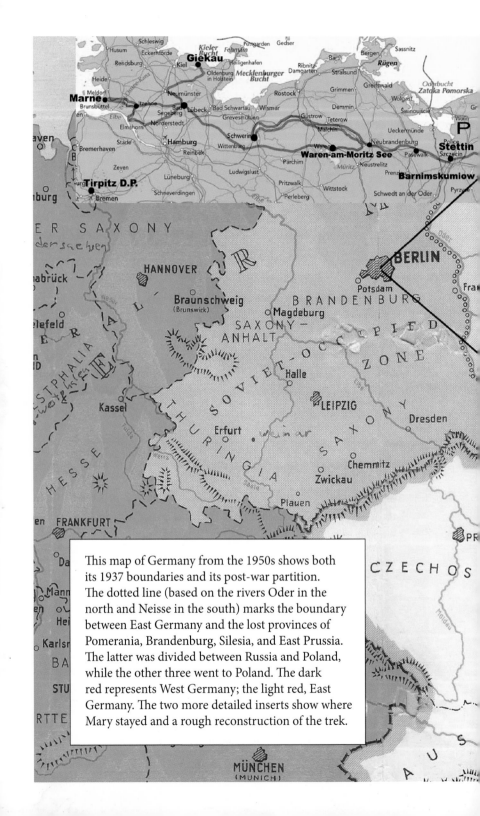

This map of Germany from the 1950s shows both its 1937 boundaries and its post-war partition. The dotted line (based on the rivers Oder in the north and Neisse in the south) marks the boundary between East Germany and the lost provinces of Pomerania, Brandenburg, Silesia, and East Prussia. The latter was divided between Russia and Poland, while the other three went to Poland. The dark red represents West Germany; the light red, East Germany. The two more detailed inserts show where Mary stayed and a rough reconstruction of the trek.

Danzig

E A S T P R U

Y

at present under Polish administration

ERANIA

N

P

O

O Posen

L

WARSAW

Bug

A

N

D

Breslau
Wrocław

Legnica

SILESIA

Jawa

Jelenia
Góra

Olawa

Brz

Wałbrzych

Świdnica

Bielawa

Langenbielau

Trutnov

Klodz

K I A

I A

VIENNA

GERMANY
in the boundaries of 1937

Towns of more than 500 000 inhabitants

○ Towns of less than 500 000 inhabitants

German boundary line of 1937

— — Boundaries of the German Federal
States

Scale ca. 1 : 3 500 000

| 50 | 0 | 50 | 100 | 150 | 200 km |
| 0 | | 50 | | 50 | 100 engl. Mi. |

Kartographie: W. Stollfuß Verlag Bonn

| 0 | 50 | 50 | 100 engl. Mi. |

1944: Jerry, Mary, and Erika in Barnimskunow

It is very strange, 60 years later, to be able to download a map on the Internet and retrace the Jentsches' walk across the fields. The long black line is the Stargard-Pyritz (Pyrzyce) train route; the train station must be the dot just to the northwest of Warnitz (Warnice), with Barnimskunow (Barnim) further down the road to the southeast. The country is no longer Germany, but Poland.

Hecker *Gut,* where Mary and the children lived in Barnimskunow before the entire village began its trek. Courtesy of Joerg Kaden

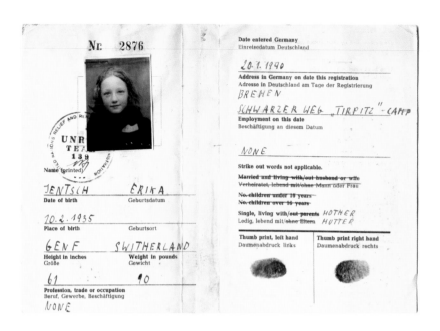

Nr. 2876

Date entered Germany
Einreisedatum Deutschland

20.1.1940

Address in Germany on date this registration
Adresse in Deutschland am Tage der Registrierung

BREHEN

SCHWARZER WEG "TIRPITZ"-CAMP

Employment on this date
Beschäftigung an diesem Datum

NONE

Name (printed)

JENTSCH   ERIKA

Date of birth   Geburtsdatum

10.2.1935

Place of birth   Geburtsort

GENF   SWITHERLAND

Height in inches   Weight in pounds
Größe   Gewicht

61   *90*

Profession, trade or occupation
Beruf, Gewerbe, Beschäftigung

NONE

Strike out words not applicable.

~~Married and living with/out husband or wife~~
~~Verheiratet, lebend mit/ohne Mann oder Frau~~

~~No. children under 16 years~~
~~No. children over 16 years~~

Single, living with/~~out parents~~   *MOTHER*
Ledig, lebend mit/~~ohne Eltern~~   *MUTTER*

Thumb print, left hand   Thumb print right hand
Daumenabdruck links   Daumenabdruck rechts

1945: Erika's identification papers for the Tirpitz Displaced Persons Camp

1945: Jerry, Mary, and Erika in Bremen after the war has ended

Season's Greetings
Dear Dada,
do you see my bangs? Very, very much love,
Erika.
P.S. Does this look like your writing?
Ich bin 2 mal "Honor girl" in unserer Klasse gewesen. Viele, viele grüße deine
Erika.
By Jerry
Lieber Dada!
hast du mein guten Anzuch gesehen?
Ich habe ein Jeep in der schuhle gemocht.
love
Gertli

Christmas, 1946: Erika writes to Gerhart: "I have been an Honor Girl in our class twice. Many many greetings, your Erika." Jerry's message says: "Dear Daddy, Have you seen my good suit? I have a jeep in school. Love, Gertli"

1958: Erica, Dieter, Hilde, and Gerhart in *Fasching*, the German Mardi Gras

city in Mecklenburg. Dora had high hopes of meeting the
trek from Caymen, their estate, and finding her mother and
mother-in-law. Most of the treks from this part of East Prussia had agreed on a rendezvous in Schwerin. They would
be well stocked with food. The boys' rapturous recital of
haunches of venison, pork, beef, and big ripe cheeses made
our mouths water. Dora spoke more soberly of tubers: tur-
nips, carrots, potatoes, and leeks. They all talked so much of
the sleigh rides through the forest lanes in glittering snow
and the Christmases on the estate and their ponies, that we
began to think of the Caymen Trek as Santa Claus with his
sleigh bringing us glorious presents of food from that cold
sparkling East Prussia. Actually Dora and I felt no hunger
pains; we had begun to live on our nerves and had enough to
eat to keep us going. And we all seemed surprisingly well.

We got a local train west that day, crowded, but we were
refreshed and in good spirits. We reached Schwerin next
morning. Dora and the two boys went right off to find the
clearinghouse for treks, while Erika, Jerry, and I trudged up
and down a large promenade in sight of an old castle. We
had agreed to meet at a bench where we had piled all our
baggage. There was a big park nearby, but of course we had
to stay with our things. Schwerin seemed to be an interesting old city. Dora and the boys came back thoroughly
discouraged. She had been from one office to another, but
no one had seen or heard of any treks from her part of East
Prussia.

We were given supper in a big hall and slept on hard
benches without straw. During an alarm we had to grope
our way in the blackness to a cellar half a block away. This,
combined with our disappointment over the Caymen Trek
and a thin cabbage soup, gave us a distaste for cities. We

vowed we'd not go near one again if we could help it.

Next morning the world looked more cheerful. It was sunny and warmer. Dora and Hermann went to another office they'd heard about and received a hopeful clue. Many East Prussian treks were definitely known to be converging on the town of Waren-am-Muritz See. They had miscalculated the time on the choked roads, and as far as we could make out were still somewhere in Vor-Pommern.

Waren was unfortunately a considerable way back east. Dora was determined to go back. Naturally she wanted to find her family. I debated what to do. I seriously considered separating from them and continuing west alone. It seemed folly for us three to retrace our steps east. But I knew absolutely no one in the West, had only the vaguest notion of the geography, and felt that my inadequate German and foreign accent were a distinct handicap. Also it didn't seem to matter much where in the West we were—we were on the right side of the Oder, out of sight and sound of the Russians. We stayed together.

We got a train east and had seats to spare. The only other passengers were groups of old men drafted at this last desperate moment into a civil guard sent east to stem the tide. They, of course, thought we were crazy—the only civilians in all Germany deliberately going east—and tried to make us turn around. Eventually, on Erika's tenth birthday, we landed in Neu Brandenburg. We went directly to the trek office where we had heartening news. "Yes, there had been some Prussische Holland treks in Neu Brandenburg. Last week some had gone through."

Dora was satisfied that she would find the Caymen outfit in Waren, which was northwest of Neu Brandenburg. As there were no trains going to Waren that day, we stayed on and celebrated Erika's birthday by going to a restaurant announcing *Reybuck* (roe-buck), unrationed. Of course it was all gone, but we had a pot roast instead—on coupons—and Dora and I each a glass of beer apiece, allowing each child a sip and Erika several. I let the birthday child wear my little fur piece. The poor child lost it, and I'm afraid I scolded her.

That night we slept in thick, clean straw in a schoolhouse. (All schools and theatres had stopped functioning, and the desks and seats had been removed to make room for the refugees.) We were so comfortable that we wouldn't budge during the two alarms but just burrowed deeper into the straw. We spent three more nights in Neu Brandenburg. Dora wasn't feeling at all well, and we couldn't get a train out anyway, so they let us stay an extra day. By then we were glad to get away, as a new influx of people came in to share our quarters in such hordes that there was no time to change the straw. Rumors had been going round of typhus, and that night we were dismayed to find fleas, which carry the fever.

We reached Waren at night, by truck and by train, about February 24. (Waren is about eighty-five miles from Stettin.) Dora was really ill now. She was doubled up under her heavy pack and knew that she had a return of her old stomach ulcers. The boys were frightened, and so was I. We were led by a sympathetic woman to a little cubbyhole in a clean barracks not far from the station, and a district nurse was found. When Dora explained that her husband was a regular officer, she was taken away with the boys to a military hospital.

Next day I found she was too ill to think of leaving, and that in a day or two they would be taken to a room outside of town until she was ready to travel. In the meantime, we had ascertained that there were no traces of any Caymen or Reussische Holland Treks in Waren. I was advised at the Refugee Office that if Frau Lilienthal would have to stay, I had better "take out residence" in Waren, otherwise we couldn't stay beyond our three days.

I was glad of a chance to settle down for a bit. We hadn't taken our boots off since Muelkenthin, due to the difficulty of getting them on again in the dark night alarms. I had to fill in large forms, giving all our past history and declaring that I was prepared to settle in Waren permanently. This I signed solemnly. We were given a slip with an address where there was a room with a stove and three beds.

It turned out to be a three-story private house on one of the corners of the picturesque central square, where there was a handsome old stone *Rathaus* (town hall). Our landlady was not over-pleased to see us, but as she had one empty room—a small, sunny space on the second floor—she was forced to take us in. There was a toilet on our floor with running water, and we had a china washbowl and pitcher in our room. It seemed very luxurious and civilized to us, and we at once bathed ourselves and washed our filthy clothes. Only now I discovered, on opening Jerry's rucksack, that at the last minute in Barnimskunow he hadn't been able to resist sneaking in a large pair of scissors. They had been slowly but inexorably cutting their way through all our wool stockings and socks. I scolded him roundly, but the scissors later came in handy.

The next day our landlady lent us a little express wagon, and we went to a store and bought a big sack of potatoes. On our return we found a cord of firewood piled on the curbstone in front of our door. This largesse proved that we were now residents of Waren-am-Muritzsee, and we were delighted with our new status. To be sure, I had to drag the wood into the cellar with the help of Erika and Jerry, but the young girl on the top floor helped me to cut it down to fit the porcelain stove that heated our room.

Late that afternoon, clean and rested, we strolled around Waren, a pretty market town set in rolling, wooded hills. Steep-roofed, half-timbered houses clustered along crooked streets that followed the course of a small river. The river flowed into Muritz Lake just outside the town, and an evergreen forest and summer cottages indicated it had once been a pleasant pre-war resort. We found Mecklenburg a fair land, too.

Within the first twenty-four hours, we realized that Waren was not the peaceful town it had seemed on that first afternoon. The town siren was installed on the *Rathaus* directly opposite our window. We had never been so near a siren, and the noise was frightful. It vibrated through every nerve and nearly split my ears. As there were four or five alarms during the day and more at night, which always meant a short *Voralarm* (warning), the prolonged *Fliegeralarm* (the real thing), and then the brief all-clear signal, it seemed that the siren was shrieking more than it was silent. I was amazed when one day Erika and Jerry came running in to say that there was a *Voralarm* at least five minutes before the siren sounded. It turned out that all the children, who were on perpetual holiday now that there was no school, had discovered that the pigeons flew out of the belfry tower at the first vibration, before the sound waves reached our ears. All shops closed during alarms, and since our milk shop, directly across the street, was only open two hours in the afternoon, those who lived near us would stand at the doors with their milk pails ready, waiting to be the first to get milk after an all-clear signal.

We were much less safe in Waren than we had been in Barnimskunow, for though there was no industry, there were cities not too far from us, and we were on the direct route to Berlin, Stettin, and cities in the southeast. Bombers were an unpredictable and baleful species. Waren was never a direct mark for the bombs, but several times raiders dropped some ballast on us on their way back.

The third floor above our room had been made into an apartment, and there lived a very simple family: an old peasant grandmother who had lived and worked all her life on a neighboring estate, her pretty middle-aged daughter whom we called Frau Hanni, and a young granddaughter of about sixteen. After the children were in bed, I'd go up and listen to the radio with them, and we'd do our mending together. The news now was almost entirely of German defeats, though toned down and minimized as much as possible. The Mecklenburgers paid little attention to the Eastern news; they were convinced the Russians would stay beyond the Oder.

At every *Voralarm* I would rush upstairs to the radio. The same calm voice briefly told us the apparent itinerary of the bombers. A large group of raiders had crossed the North Sea five minutes before at Cuxhaven, headed toward Pinneberg. They were now over Ratzeburg and heading for Hagenow. No! They had swerved south of Ludwigslust and were speeding toward Perleburg. Like Paul Revere's ride: if they were seen over Hagenow, they would take the northern route toward Parchim and fly over Waren. If they passed over Ludwigslust, they were on the southern route but would still go over us. When we heard the beautiful name of Salzwedel, we knew we were safe this time, for that was the turning point for the southeast route, and we could go on about our business. If it had been one of the first two, we reluctantly would have gone to the cellar, really only a tiny mud hole for storing wood and potatoes.

The old grandmother would tell us stories of life on the *Graf's* estate. He was now an officer in the army, and they had all liked him but not his wife. The old lady hesitated a moment, then "*Die Frau Gräfin ist Amerikanerin, aber nicht so nett wie Sie.*" ("The Count's wife is an American, but not as nice as you.") I ran down and got my address book. It was the American *Gräfin* from Boston, where Jane was staying! I'd forgotten all about her. I gathered they were very wealthy and that the estate was large and the castle enormous. I immediately wrote to Jane, saying couldn't we meet someday soon in Waren.

Incredible as it seems to me now, the post was still functioning. I had written to my sister-in-law, Lonny Jentsch, and to a friend of Frau Wegener's in Berlin. To my joy I heard immediately from both and learned that Lonny and Else were both alive. Her friend wrote that Else, after many weeks of terror and hardship, had landed in Vor-Pommern in a tiny village by the sea.

Not long after I'd written, I received a surprise visit from Jane, who had driven into town with the *Gräfin* to take two of the latter's daughters to the dentist. Jane and her two little boys were getting on well, though the castle was swarming with relatives of the *Graf*. She didn't see much of the *Gräfin*, who was temperamental, but they intended to stay there for the duration. I saw them all off in their smart equipage with two mettlesome horses, but I was no longer envious of Jane. We were getting along just as well.

About a week after Dora had entered the hospital, Hermann and Lütti had come to find us and tell us she had been discharged and they were all living with a family in one of the cottages on the lake. They were in fine fettle now that their mother was better and were having the time of their lives in the woods. We were somewhat envious but promised to walk out to spend the day soon. It was a forty-five minute walk, and there were too many alarms, so we visited only twice. But Dora was getting better daily, thanks to a good bed, rest, and some special milk she was given. The boys had been in to inquire about the trek, but there was no sign of it, and Dora reluctantly gave up any idea of making contact with it. She could only hope that they were safe somewhere.

I took the children on walks through the town and outside to a wooded hill nearby. We felt safe in the woods and only flattened out under the trees when we saw the American planes directly over us. Spring was just beginning here, a shy, cool spring with Easter almost upon us. Inspired by my friends upstairs, I saved some flour and sugar and mixed a *Streuselkuchen*. On Maundy Thursday I joined the procession of women walking down the street, each carefully holding a baking tin covered with a clean napkin, all going to the baker's. It was the custom in the small towns—not in the country or in the villages—to take your baking to the baker's great ovens, where the women stood around waiting for their turn, chatting and gossiping. The cakes all came out beautifully browned, even mine.

Right after Easter, toward the end of our sixth week in Waren, Dora was able to walk in to see us. She looked very thin but felt much better. Since the British and Americans seemed to be marching east now, and Waren was in their path, we decided to stay on. I preferred to be taken by my countrymen, but if the British were on this route instead, it was okay by me and Dora.

The Waren newspaper had ceased publication before we got there, but it printed one daily war bulletin and pasted it on the office window. Every day I walked down to read it, for often we couldn't get the radio news because of the bombing raids. One morning I was horrified to read that the Russians had crossed the Oder and taken Stettin. I couldn't believe it! We were considerably nearer the Oder than the vague (to me) Western Front. Next morning my worst fears were confirmed. For some inexplicable reason, the Americans and British had changed course and instead of heading toward Waren were going far south of us. The Russians were free to swarm through Mecklenburg, taking us as they went west.

I hastened out toward Dora's house and met her coming in. She too, had heard. After a hasty consultation, we decided to move on. We had come this far to escape the Russians, and we would not be caught now. We learned that in a town not far to the north of us there was still one train a day going west. When we told Frau Hanni our decision she threw up her hands: It was suicide to leave. We'd be taken on the road, maybe in open fighting, by the "others" and what was the difference? They were all enemies. I said it was perhaps no different for the Mecklenburgers, but they didn't yet know the Russians. We did. She said that everyone knew there was famine in the West, particularly in Holstein, but though the thought of starvation was grim, the Russians were grimmer. We knew we had to go.

There was one bit of official red tape we had to undergo. As we had taken out residence papers, we now had to sign off. We were told we couldn't leave without doing this, but

initially Dora and I just laughed. How would they know
we'd left, and what would they do if we did? It turned out
that they'd confiscate our potatoes and wood, instead of let-
ting us give them to whomever we wished. We signed off.
I deeded my worldly goods and possessions to Frau Hanni
and posted a final hasty note to Lonny and Else.

At the office they asked us where we were going, a question we hadn't expected. Dora and I had vaguely decided
on Schleswig-Holstein. It was perhaps the most refugee-in-
fested spot in the West, but it was not in the mainstream of
the fighting armies. Also there were few large cities, especially industrial ones, and we wanted above all else to avoid
big cities. We were country people and distrusted cities: too
many people, too many bombs, too little food.

We both said we were going to Schleswig-Holstein. They
repeated what we heard daily: it was crowded with no place
to stay and perhaps starvation. We were quite surprised
that they seemed to want us to stay in Waren. But I think
it was now the official policy, probably a wise one, to try
and make people stay put as the war ended. Then the man
looked sternly at us and said, "You know you cannot leave
here without a paper from someone at your chosen destination promising you shelter." This was unforeseen. But to
my astonishment, Dora nonchalantly produced a battered
looking postcard. "Why, we're going to Marne in Schleswig
on the North Sea. I have cousins there." The old man put on
his spectacles and read the card. Without another word he
signed us off as residents of Waren-am-Muritzsee.

It seems that Dora had saved this old card from some
cousins who had gone to Marne early in the war, because
of the address in the West. While I was talking to the man
about the possibility of going to Lake Constance, Dora had

scribbled in pencil on the postcard: "Do come to Marne. We have room for all six of you." I'm sure the official saw through it but thought it didn't matter any longer. So now we were off to Marne (pronounced "Marnuh") on the North Sea. The name was pretty, and I had never seen the North Sea: two very good reasons for going.

As I started packing, I discarded the most worn-out of our clothes. A week before, Dora and I had been told that as refugees we were entitled to go to a room and get some old garments stored there for us *Flüchtlinge* (literally one who flees). These were old clothes given by the German populace during the frequent drives during the war. In the early years, both Dora and I had contributed. It was a discouraging assortment, well picked over before we arrived. Dora found a pair of pants for Lütti, a couple of shirts for Hermann, and a darned wool skirt. I found an old black silk skirt, a pair of heavy brown corduroy boy's knickerbockers for Erika, and two men's starched-bosomed dress shirts for Jerry, which he used for nightshirts for a year. Both children had either outgrown or worn out practically everything. We could find no shoes.

We started out early in the morning of April 9. As we had to walk several miles, Frau Hanni's daughter and a boy Erika's age helped us carry our suitcases part of the way. Once more the warning: "*Ich wäre so gerne geblieben, Aber der wagen der rollt.*" How I would like to stay, but the coach rolls on. No one knew when the end of the war would come—in days or in weeks or even months. Where were the Allies exactly, and would we meet fighting on the road? It was a long walk to the train, but we were fit again.

We got on the train after not too long a wait and found that our fellow passengers were Mecklenburgers in flight from the Eastern towns we had left not so long ago. Their speech had a special singing quality, a gay lilt, very different from the speech of Pommern, though all North Germany spoke "low" German. The train seemed to be filled almost entirely with excited children and feather beds.

So began the second half of our trek: more two- or three-night stands sleeping in straw; more soup, bread, and coffee doled out to us by tired women and girls. It was getting warmer and our heavy clothes weighed us down, but we still flung ourselves down on the straw wearing all our clothes and even our boots. More and more alarms sounded day and night, as we zigzagged our way west, sometimes by train, sometimes by truck, sometimes on foot.

The trains would start bravely off, be held at the next station during an alarm, start dispiritedly on, and then bog down in a field because of mechanical breaks or lack of coal dust. From Waren to Marne in a straight line on the map seems to be about 165 miles, but we must have covered five times that.

We usually tried to find a corner in the straw where we all six could stretch out together. Stumbling dead-tired into a schoolhouse, we piled our suitcases about us, and with our heads on our rucksacks slept soundly, often throughout alarms. It was such a chore to rouse the children and grope our way through a dark, unfamiliar street to the shelter and then back again several times during the night. Most small towns did not have cellars in schoolhouses, and the nearest shelter was never very near. The straw we slept on now was tired, too, and typhus-infested. For all these Germans, the end was near and the enemy was at hand. They fed us refugees, but there wasn't any more fresh straw, and if they pointed out the shelters, they were not responsible for our seeking safety if we didn't want to go. As the war ground to its end, people became more and more reckless. Some sold their bread and meat for cigarettes. I had never realized how much our Western civilization depended on stimulants until there were none. Coffee, tea, alcohol, tobacco: if we had just had had one of these occasionally, life would have been easier.

The most tragic aspect of this great migration—and even now when I write about it I feel a chill of horror—was the lost children. Every house wall, boarding fence, in every village, town, or city we passed through was covered with short pathetic messages, in chalk, pencil, or bits of paper pasted on. "Hans Kruger, eight years old, lost somewhere between Rostock and Gistow January 31. His mother Frau Lisbeth Kruger now in Schwerin." Or "Barbi Schmidt, age three and a half, lost in Passewalk, Pommern; her mother Frau Ilse Schmedt now in Lübeck." Or "Franz Schultz, aged six, his sister Anna in Segeberg." Very occasionally, such a message as: "Four-year old boy calling himself Ricki found on the road between Bad Kleinen and Kasenow, East Prussian dialect." There must have been a thousand. I was so thankful my children were old enough to walk. Mothers with several children, one in arms and the others very small, were those to be pitied most. They couldn't keep track of all the children all the time.

In one town we got in about 10 p.m. The dimly-lit station waiting room was very large with some benches and not too crowded. So after our supper, we came back there instead of staying in the crowded movie theatre. In one corner were some fleeing Frenchmen, sitting round a table. I went up and talked to them in French. They had come from Brandenburg, just northeast of Berlin. Their old wagon had broken down, and they were hoping to get a train. They knew nothing more than we did as to the course of the war. For some reason this encounter stands out in my memory, perhaps because the vast hall was full of dark, dramatic shadows, and talking with the Frenchmen in a German station seemed strange.

Our flight now became just a list of names—Bad Oldesloe, Segeberg, Elmshorn, and many others—memorable only for their good or bad sleeping quarters and under what air route they lay. We no longer knew the days of the week or month. We knew only that we were going west, if by a slow and devious way. If we heard of a train or truck going on, we'd try for it, which meant that often we found ourselves too far south and next time we'd be north without having gained much ground toward the West. Our chief object was to keep north of Hamburg and on across the Schleswig-Holstein peninsula until we came to Marne on the North Sea.

Rumors were buzzing all around us, but as we never had access to a radio, we knew nothing for sure. Some said there was a great battle going on in Hamburg, that the British were cutting us off from Lübeck. We saw no British or American soldiers or fighting of any kind. But Dora and I were more and more anxious to reach Marne as soon as possible. The children were good, but we were all in a dazed condition, all living on our nerves. So many places, so many people! Dora and I had each had about nine hundred marks apiece when we started out. As we had spent none for fare, and only a little for our food and rent in Waren, we had most of it left. We decided to pool our money and do the same with our new ration cards when we reached Marne. All four children were in the same category for food, which made it simple.

The last few days had introduced a new worry into our already crowded lives: the *Tiefflieger* or dive-bomber. People pointed them out to us from trucks or train windows. They looked so harmless, just one single plane, that they made only a dim impression on our consciousness. We were preoccupied with our effort to reach the haven of Marne before the war ended, which, according to all the rumors we heard, might be any day now. Our main object was to be under a "permanent" roof, far from a big city when that happened.

When we landed in Elmshorn late one night, we congratulated ourselves with a deep sigh of relief. The worst was over. We no longer feared the Russians; we had left them far behind. We were actually in Schleswig-Holstein, west of Lubeck and well north of Hamburg.[12] We consented to go to the bunker with good grace that night, though it was a horrid little one with no light. One phobia from the war has still remained with me: darkness. It is terrifying to hear the alarm and the sound of bombers while groping in total blackness in a strange place. I was never without a candle-end and matches after Berlin, and even now, fourteen years later, I always carry a small flashlight in my purse.

The next afternoon we got ourselves to Glückstadt on the Elbe, a short ride west, and then we would go north for a change—north to Marne and the North Sea.

We were up on the Glückstadt platform early the next day to get the first train north (if there was one). On the map, as the crow flies, Marne is only about thirty-five miles northwest of Glückstadt. It was a sparkling spring morning, and our spirits were high. The children couldn't keep still.

---

[12] The Second Russian Army reached the Baltic on May 2 and on May 3 took Hamburg.

Erika asked me the usual question, "Mamu, what does your instinct tell you today?"

After our custom, established probably in Stettin, this meant, "In case of *Fliegeralarm* do we go into a shelter or stay up on the platform and try for a train?" I rarely hesitated to answer promptly. I was far from sure myself, but I realized that a decisive answer gave them a feeling of security, and the good luck we had had thus far sustained my role of oracle. I said now, without hesitation, "We stay up." We were sure the auguries were good today. A train drew in, and we piled on just as a *Voralarm* sounded. The train pulled out and we were soon in the country. It was crowded, and we were all scattered in different compartments, since Dora and I always pushed the children in first and then scrambled on ourselves wherever we could.

We were trundling slowly along through the flat, open country when someone in my compartment pointed to the sky. "*Tiefflieger!*" I saw one silvery speck far up. In a second it had swooped down on us, and instantly there was a loud explosion and the cars rattled and crashed together. Doors were flung open and we all leaped out, scrambling down and up deep wide ditches on each side of the track. I grabbed two children in my compartment and dragged them with me. Everyone was streaming over the fields, yelling "Flatten out, flatten out!" I flung the strange children down, myself on top of them. We heard another explosion, screams, and then more grindings and clashings. Then dead silence for about five minutes.

"He's gone!" someone said, and we got up, dazed. I looked around frantically for Erika and Jerry but saw neither them nor the Lilienthals. As doors of most European train compartments open on both sides of the car, there were people spread out on both sides of the track. I shepherded the two children to the largest group of people and then began searching, but the occupants of our train had spread themselves over half a mile of fields, wandering now to various nearby farmhouses. Our locomotive had been hit. I could only hope my children were safe with some stranger.

As I kept searching for them, I saw that many people were gathered some distance away in front of the nearest farmhouse. I was overjoyed to find not only Jerry and Erika, but the Lilienthals, who had all been looking for me. The few who had been wounded were inside and were being taken care of. We were given drinks of water while we rested on the grass.

After some two hours we saw another locomotive brought up and coupled to the cars. Only two cars had been damaged, those nearest the engine. The train crew finally waved and shouted to us, and we all piled on board We were on our way again, not without some nervousness. It was an ill-fated journey. Within half an hour, another menacing silver speck appeared. It plummeted down and demolished our second engine.

When a third locomotive was brought up in an hour's time, many people had had enough and refused to get on the train again. But we six grimly decided to stick it out, and off we puffed again. We were all nervous and jittery now, especially when the Kiel Canal came in sight. It was quite a long bridge we had to cross, and if a dive-bomber chose to attack us then, there would be no hope.

No one spoke as we crawled along until we were safe on the other side. Eventually we pulled up to the terminal called Itzehöe, a strange and intriguing name, sounding to me very un-German. Perhaps it was Danish, from when

Schleswig-Holstein had been part of Denmark. Unbelievable as it seems, everyone found all his own baggage, nothing lost or stolen. After a few hours there, we boarded a local going west to Marne, and we all vowed we'd never leave Marne nor get on another train until after the war. The distance between Glückstadt and Marne was only about forty miles, but it had encompassed enough excitement to last a lifetime.

It was very late when we arrived, and we had a long walk from the station into the little town. We stumbled into the schoolhouse straw and slept until we were awakened by our bedfellows getting up. We sniffed in the salt air, liking the smell of our new home. We washed the children and ourselves as well as we could under the usual cold-water tap in the little basin.

This washing process on our flight was always a source of wonder to me. No matter how late they had come in, or how tired they were, the German mothers always scrubbed their children every night or morning. Dora and I saw that our brood's hands were clean, and sometimes their faces, but we were too lazy to attempt more. It was a great comfort to find the privies clean. The less primitive johns in the stations and cities were not so well kept. Scarcity of newspapers or any kind of paper was one of our worst trials, and we saved every scrap we could get hold of.

After a rather poor breakfast, Dora and the boys went to find the cousins outside of town, and we three Jentsches went to the refugee bureau to get ourselves a room and become residents of Marne. It was the first brusque, unfriendly office we had encountered. There was no room; they were more than overflowing with our ilk; and so, far from becoming residents, we would have to move on after two more nights. I pleaded with them, telling our story and stressing the *Tieffliegers* we had encountered. This was an old tale to them and they remained adamant. We walked about the town and heard rumors of a big coup. They expected a combined naval-and-air battle in the next few days, and German supplies were already converging on Marne. This didn't make us any happier as we wandered through the streets. The Lilienthals came back after a long, hot walk equally discouraged. The cousins were no longer there. We had all of us already made up our minds about this place that was to have been our snug haven: a dull, flat, uninteresting little town with undistinguished architecture and inhospitable inhabitants. It was not even on the sea. The surrounding country was flat and marshy with irrigation canals. Two more nights we ate the pallid cabbage soup. The other refugees were complaining and aggrieved, too. No one liked Marne. But we didn't give up looking for rooms, anywhere, to await the end. We didn't fancy taking part in a big battle, but it seemed too late to find any roof anywhere else.

On our last morning, returning from the refugee bureau, we accosted a friendly-looking young officer. Did he know of any place we could go? I remember adding "a pretty place." He looked astonished, scratched his head, and finally said, "Well, how about Plön? I used to visit my aunt there as a boy. It's very pretty. On a lake with a fine castle." Where was Plön? "Oh, northeast from here across Holstein." We thanked him and he wished us luck.

At the station we found out that we would have to take the local train back to Itzehöe and strike out northeast from there. I balked. I couldn't face more dive-bombers. They all pointed out to me, even Jerry, that they wouldn't let us stay in Marne. There was no alternative. We went the long way back to our quarters to get our baggage and then got a train to Itzehöe, where we arrived shortly and without mishap, glad to be out of Marne.

In Itzehöe we learned there were no more trains running: too many had been destroyed. We were told that military trucks were numerous, and if we went out on the road toward Segeberg we'd surely find one going in our direction. (These trucks were ordered to take on refugees heading in the same direction if they were flagged at a crossroad.)

It started raining as we trudged along. A truck picked us up at last. We clambered over the high tail and started on a novel and terrifying tour of Holstein, lasting for at least four days in various trucks. We zigzagged across the country at a terrific pace, jolting and bumping and careening around curves.

The *Tieffliegers* were after us once more. They patrolled all roads as well as rails. To his mother's horror, Hermann sat on top of one truck's cab to spot the bombers. When one appeared, the brakes screeched and we scrambled out as best we could, trying to reach the ridiculously shallow foxholes hastily dug along the sides of the road. We were lucky when we were hidden by hedgerows or trees. Usually we got at least our heads in the holes. The worst was jumping out of or climbing into the high trucks. We were so clumsy in our winter clothes. The *Tieffliegers* were doing a thorough job. Demolished trucks lay along all the roads, some still smoking, and our only thought was to get under a roof and stay put.

Sometimes we waited for hours at a crossroad after being abandoned by a truck that had to turn off in another direction. We landed once at a town called Kellinghusen— it had a nice Irish sound to me—and tried to hole up there but were forced on again. We learned to be glad when it was cloudy or rainy, because there was less chance of the dive-bombers seeing us. Those reckless four days seemed a fortnight at least. We lost all sense of direction and sometimes found ourselves back in a town we had visited two days before. The idea was to keep moving even if in the wrong direction. I remember the names of Segeburg, Bad Bramstedt, and, last, the city of Neumünster.

Finally, we reached the picturesque town of Plön on a wooded slope overlooking the Plönersee with its imposing medieval castle on a high hill. We couldn't have told you what the Holstein landscape was like on our wild truck travels, but now we saw that here it was wooded and hilly and all clothed in fresh spring green. Plön was a pretty place and a small one, though it had once been a Danish provincial capital. For nearly a week we stayed in another schoolhouse, small and flimsy, near the foot of the castle hill.

Dora and I, belligerent with desperation, haunted the tired Refugee Office personnel several times a day, trying to get a room, but there wasn't one in the whole of Plön. Because the schoolhouse was as flimsy as it was conspicuous, we were told to spend our nights in the castle dungeons. Every night we climbed up the steep hill to the dark, cold, vaulted keep, a labyrinth of halls and little rooms and passageways, with perhaps a thousand other people from Plön. We felt like night crawlers as we stumbled around, trying to find a dry corner. It was safe, but it was very uncomfortable with a few benches (not nearly enough) and no straw. Dora and her boys lugged their two heavy suitcases up and down every day, but I took only our rucksacks and my briefcase and left our heavy cases in the schoolhouse.

We continued to make ourselves disagreeable to the head of the Refugee Office until he hated the sight of us. If they couldn't get us a room here, they must find us a place nearby at once. Tomorrow. Today. Now! On the morning of April 27 they positively beamed at us, telling us to be on the freight platform at one o'clock sharp. A train would take us to a village where they had found us rooms.

We were on the spot a good three hours early in a drenching rain. At one-thirty a little train of three or four boxcars backed out of the freight yard, and we were told to hop on. We did, along with a few hundred others, the last remnants of the Eastern refugees. We had no idea in what direction we were going. We had grasped the slip of paper with the name Neuhaus on it without thinking to ask where it was, but we knew it was in the country. "They" had found us a room and if people tried to put us out, well it was "their" funeral; we had a magic slip of paper to prove it.

Four hours and forty-two miles later, we reached the end of the line. "Lütjenburg. All out!" A lovely sight met our eyes. Waiting outside the small station were comfortable farm wagons lined with hay. As we tumbled off the train, farmers called: "Who's for Gadendorf?" or "Who's for Malente?" and at last (in a good, strong Holstein accent) "Here for Neuhaus!" It was the smallest of the wagons with only one horse, but he was stout and sleek. We climbed aboard with one other family: two women, several children, and a flimsy crate of hens that promptly escaped into the good clean hay.

We drove off along cobbled shady streets through the old Holstein market town with houses of mellow red brick, all very neat and prim. As we left the town, Dora and I looked at each other and smiled, our first spontaneous and relaxed smile for a month. When the farmer told us we had seventeen kilometers to go, we nestled down in our hay and the children began to sing, anything, everything, but especially the old Williams College songs and "Lord Jeffrey Amherst," which I had taught our four along the way. (One of my favorite relatives, Uncle Sam Hutchings, had been a Williams College man and had taught me the songs in my childhood.)

The "chicken children," as Lütti called the strange family with us, joined in to the outrage of Hermann. "They think they're singing English," he muttered. "They don't know what a single word means!" His English was excellent. He had a natural aptitude and had received very good instruction in the Königsberg schools. Lütti, on the other hand, didn't care a hoot about learning English, except a few slang words, but he mimicked us to perfection.

The rain came down harder than ever, but we didn't care. The road ran between rows of trees, curving around the rolling hills through very appealing country. There were big farms, fertile fields, and meadows dotted with great oaks spreading shade for the herds of Holstein cows. Everywhere was the soft bloom of spring. There was no traffic except for two wagons far ahead, but there were several wrecked trucks and wagons, the work of dive-bombers. I noticed a sign at a long road leading west: *Gottesgabe* (God's gift). Our driver said it was a big *Gut*, one of the oldest estates in the region. It was such a romantic name I wished we were going there instead of to Neuhaus.

We turned off the high road at an old post inn and a store, called Seekrug, and followed a country lane to the right. We had been going northwest but now turned directly east. We passed one end of a large lake, Selentersee, and skirted a beech wood, where razor-backed hogs were snuffling for truffles and beechnuts. After two kilometers, we rounded a bend and saw a large *Gut* with a seventeenth-century castle but no village. From the lake we saw formal gardens and terraces, but our wagon turned to the other side where an avenue of trees led to a huge *Hof.* "Neuhaus," said the farmer, pulling up at the gate. We were awed. How exciting to live in a castle! But just as we were about to climb down, a man came out and spoke to the farmer, who nodded, flicked his whip, and drove past. We shouted that this was where we were going and waved our slips. "Nein," he told us. "No room. We go on to Giekau."

It was dusk now, and though we were tired and subdued, we were not disheartened. We knew he had to take us somewhere. Another half-mile and it was dark. We had driven eight miles. We turned a corner and here was Giekau, a tiny village with a big, old church, its high square tower dwarfing the cottages clustered round it under the big trees. This was all we could see as we climbed out in front of the smallest schoolhouse we had yet seen. The tiny room was piled deep with the cleanest, freshest smelling straw, and there was an electric light burning. (Of course the windows were blacked out.) While we went to a beautifully clean privy and washed ourselves ceremoniously in honor of the general spotlessness, some women had set up a trestle table near the door and were piling a feast on it: big pitchers of fresh warm milk, fresh bread with thick slices of cheese, and an apple apiece!

The ministering angels introduced themselves as the Frau Pastor, the Frau Förster, and the Frau Leherin. They were, as the German implies, the wives of the pastor, the forester and the schoolteacher, and they plied us with food.

All the children grabbed for second helpings of bread and cheese, but the ladies assured us there was plenty. They even administered aspirin to Dora and me, and a cup of tea to one of the two other women, who was old and exhausted. As they left us in our snug bed, they told us we would be taken to our rooms in the morning, and that in case of *Fliegeralarm* the school bell would ring and we were to run across the street into the church. We nodded sleepily, but none of us had the slightest intention of obeying such a childish warning as a school bell. We felt far too comfortable and safe. We all slept blissfully and were only awakened about nine o'clock by the cackling of the hens outside in their crate.

The ladies came in with our breakfast, and after we had washed and eaten, an official delegation arrived. The Herr Burgermeister, the Herr Förster, and the Herr Pastor! We wondered if they were all going to make speeches to welcome us to Giekau. After greeting us pleasantly, the Chicken Family were told to gather up their things and they would be guided to their quarters just outside the village. Then the Herr Förster spoke up, looking rather nervous (he was a shy man anyway). They were extremely sorry, but there just wasn't any room for us in Giekau. Neuhaus had been expected to take us in and, when they didn't, Giekau had agreed to house us for the night, but there really was no corner in the village for us.

The children looked at Dora and me fearfully. Then we both said at once that we were sorry, but we had to stay. We had been wandering for three months with four children and now at last headquarters in Plön had promised us rooms here. They all looked extremely uncomfortable. Frau Pastor Harms and Frau Förster Jaeger were called back and consulted, but everyone shook their heads. They explained that the *Pfarrhaus* (although in this part of Germany, they called it the *Pastorat*) was big, but they already had thirty strangers there. The *Förster's* house was almost as large, and they too had twenty. The Mayor's house was small but was filled to overflowing, and the rest of the village was made up of a few small cottages, also full. Also the outlying farms.

Dora immediately asked why the Küchen Familie had found quarters. They had been sent to what was practically a chicken-coop, said the *Förster,* and they couldn't put us in such a place, if it were available, which it was not. The *Burgermeister* would inquire into the neighboring villages, and perhaps…but we shook our heads.

"No, we will have to stay here," we said firmly. And then Dora said, "And what's more, we'll stay together, even if it's in a cow-stall." A long silence. Then Frau Pastor Harms spoke up briskly. "Very well. I'll put my boys in the larder if necessary and give these poor people their room." She did. We stayed and raised the number of strangers in her house to thirty-six. This was just two weeks short of the general German surrender.

Chapter Six

EAST HOLSTEIN
April to November 1945
Strange Interlude

ADOLF HITLER, WITH EVA BRAUN, committed suicide in the Berlin bunker on April 30, 1945. Their corpses were taken out into the garden, where, in accordance with Hitler's last wishes, they were set afire. Fortunately, another of Hitler's final wishes was not carried out. On March 19th he had issued an order demanding that all military, industrial, transportation, and communication installations be destroyed, along with all the stores in Germany, to keep them from falling into enemy hands. Albert Speer, Minister for Armament and War Production, opposed the directive and refused to execute it. If he had, millions inside Germany would have starved. Hitler's reason for the order, he told Speer, was that "those who will remain after the battle are only the inferior ones, for the good ones have been killed."

We loved Giekau on sight, and we liked Frau Harms and Frau Jaeger from the first moment we saw them. They were friendly and understanding, and above all they "spoke our language." That first night we congratulated ourselves with pardonable pride. We had chosen this perfect refuge out of all Germany. We had rejected Marne and gotten here on our own, and we were here to stay. The small discomforts were as nothing to the sympathetic atmosphere we felt. Fear and anxiety were forgotten.

The two Harms boys, Siebrandt and Peter, had removed their belongings from the "garden room," formerly the dining room, and we were in full possession. The outdoors pervaded it, a damp earthy smell and a dim green gloom from branches swaying against the windows. The French doors opened onto the orchard, and it was alight with the white froth of apple trees in bloom.

We stuffed four pallets with clean straw for the children. The only free bed left in the house was an old iron double bed with sagging, lumpy springs that Dora and I had to share. We had a washstand and a bureau, two chairs and some crates. Eventually we got a kitchen table. Frau Harms gave us three sheets, an old comforter, and a blanket to supplement our assorted travel rugs. We were installed in a couple of hours.

The *Pastorat* was much larger than the *Pfarrhaus* in Barnimskunow, but well proportioned. In the early nineteenth century they built their parsonages spaciously to serve as parish houses as well. Visiting church dignitaries were put up, and often the county nurse made it her headquarters. Our *Pastorat* was of soft red brick with a white portico. The Giekauer church was a tall square tower of the same red brick with a graceful white belfry, and the rest of the church stretched out behind. Pastor Harms was the shepherd of a large parish, which included the countryside and several neighboring villages. Neuhaus was the nearest estate, nearly a mile away.

Giekau is a tiny hamlet on a slight, wooded rise sloping down to a large lake, Selenter See. Its dozen cottages are scattered along two country, cobbled roads at right angles to each other, with a few farms and cottages opening on to branching dirt roads. Near the *Pastorat* is an irregular village green with big oaks. Like the rest of the German countryside, Holstein is organized regionally. Giekau's importance lies in its towering church and its imposing modern dairy. It also has a *Burgermeister*. All of these serve a region, probably the same boundary as the older parish. But there is no butcher, baker, or general store. We bought bread and dry groceries in Dransau, two miles northwest of us, and we had to walk eight miles in the other direction to Lütjenburg for our meat.

The Förster's house was older than the *Pastorat*, with mullioned windows and narrow, winding passages. Down a leafy lane, beyond a low stone wall, it nestled against the Neuhaus Forest on a little hill overlooking the lake. The old profession of forester in Germany carries weight and social dignity. It is usually carried on from father to son. Our *Förster*, with the happy name of *Jäger* (Hunter), was a man of parts, and he and his wife were well liked in the neighborhood. They were both rather shy and conservative, but kind and friendly. There was much running back and forth between the *Forsterei* and the *Pastorat*, as the two families were great friends. Waldtraut Jäger, two years older than Erika, was a quiet, dark, long-legged girl with a twinkle in her eye, and her brother Jochen, round and brown and merry, became fast friends with Jerry.

Herr Burgermeister Gries (the mayor) lived with his family up another lane. They were not included more than was absolutely necessary in the social life of the parish, as they were neither attractive nor interesting. I think he had been put in by the Nazi regime. But, of course, all the children in the village played together. The daughter Erika's age had the incongruous name of Cristl Gries. Fortunately she has since changed it, as she later married a G.I. and now lives in Texas. Besides the farmers and the blacksmith, there was the young schoolteacher, then in the army, but his wife also taught and lived in a small house next to the school with her child.

The Holstein villages are closer together than those in Pommern, but hidden by hills and trees. There were many large estates, and smaller, independent farms scattered about. It was much less feudal here, and the farm laborers usually owned their own cottages. The estate owners seemed pleasant, but life was too busy for me to ever know them well. They sometimes dropped in to the *Pastorat* for a call or on parish business when they had errands in Lütjenburg and a horse could be spared, for they were all devoted to the Harms family.

European country life is primitive, even in normal times, but one quickly gets used to it. It is the life our grandparents lived. In Germany or France, except in the big cities, I have never lived nor visited in a house with central heating. Behind our orchard were the little stable, the barn, and the privies. The latter situation at the *Pastorat* was now acute, as can be imagined, with all us refugees. The emptying and cleaning had become an Augean stables situation. There were no longer any farmhands, so the Harms boys took it on, and now Hermann and Lütti were their unwilling helpers.

For the first few days, before we could get our new ration cards, we were the guests of the Harms and the Jägers. While the Lilienthals were eating at the *Pastorat*, the Jentschs were dining at the *Forsterei*, and the next day was reversed. Looking back on it, they were extraordinarily gracious to their uninvited guests. We took it as our due at the time. Dora and I agreed to pay Frau Harms thirty marks between us for our room, per month.

This situation in West Germany of the unwilling host and the reluctant *Flüchtlinge* is hard to believe in America. It was a staggering proposition: to house millions of women and children in the most crowded third of Germany, where the housing shortage had already been acute since long before the war, and where now the almost total destruction of the cities and towns had made refugees of several million West Germans before we Easterners had even left home. Many of the early refugees from the Western cities had taken some household goods with them to the country, but all of us from the East arrived with only what we had on our backs. By 1944 nothing, absolutely nothing, could be replaced. So the host had to furnish us with everything— linen, cooking utensils, dishes. And this meant giving them to us. They were old to begin with, and we finished them off. Frau Harms gave us, beside the bedding, two or three towels and one large cook-pot, and we had to be grateful.

The whole *Flüchtlinge* problem worsened as time went on and reached its peak after I left Germany, when, before the rubble had been cleared and new building could begin, it was realized that the refugees from the East, eight million of them forming one-sixth of the population of West Germany, were in the West to stay. It didn't ease until seven or eight years after the war was over.

The material side was difficult enough, but the psychological problem of so many ill-assorted women living unwillingly together in the most unbelievably confined proximity was unprecedented in the Western world. It was slum living, but thank God Germans tend to be obsessively clean. Whole families in one room, two or three in a bed. Grandmothers and little children sleeping together, a mother and a teen-age daughter in one bed with three assorted boys on pallets in the same room. And all dressing together, all eating their meals together in that one room.

In winter and stormy weather it was, of course, worse. The *Flüchtlinge* were often unreasonable and demanding, and the hosts as frequently unsympathetic and hard. The worst situations arose when the standards and backgrounds were very different. Sometimes the more educated and worldly made the most adaptable guests and hosts. But not always. The farmers' wives showed up very well. Of course, the *Flüchtlinge* were often quarrelsome among themselves, and family relations were frequently at a high tension point.

I marveled, though, at how adaptable and cheerful most of the people were most of the time, both hosts and guests. On the whole our fellow inmates were friendly and helpful—one couldn't expect them all to be congenial—and we were all extremely lucky to have landed in the *Pastorat*. Perhaps the hardest thing for every one of us to bear was that no one was ever alone, not even for a minute.

Lotte Harms was generous and sympathetic and had the imagination to see our point of view when she was most irritated at our demands or complaints. She liked people, and she liked us. Herr Pastor Theodor Harms (Fejor to his wife) stemmed from the flat, Frisian coast. He was a tall, stooped, scholarly man, witty as well as kind and benevolent, and very popular. Not unlike John Foster Dulles in appearance, he seemed much older than he was. He, too, was kind and sympathetic to us, but of course Lotte ran the household.

Lotte, or "Frau Pastorat" as we all called her, was a very attractive woman, intelligent, vigorous and impulsive. Thirteen years younger than her husband, she was a native of the Hertz but had lived all her married life in Giekau. Crisp, curly, dark hair, pleasantly graying, set off her brown, heart-shaped face with its short, straight nose. Her mouth was exceptionally pretty, and her face was rarely still. This mobility of expression and her bright hazel eyes were her greatest charm, sometimes warm, sometimes sharp, most often quizzical. One never knew what she was thinking. She hated housework but loved her garden and did a man's work out of doors.

She took care of her enormous vegetable garden and orchard single-handedly and raised a goat and three Merino sheep. She sheared the sheep herself, carding and spinning the wool, lovely, rough, strong stuff. In more leisurely times she knit socks, stockings, and sweaters for the family, friends, and villagers, including two very handsome costumes for her daughter and herself in the natural colors, cream, brown, and black. The goat was a comic supplement from which Frau Harms theoretically got additional milk, but she was more trouble than she was worth.

Frauke, their oldest child, about seventeen and very pretty, was a slim, elusive girl with an ethereal quality. But her Puckish, mischievous air, like her mother's, and her terse, humorous phrases soon belied the medieval role I had at first assigned to her. Siebrandt and Peter were sturdy, dark country boys. Peter, the youngest, and Lütti were of an age, had similar interests, and got along very well. Siebrandt and Hermann were not so congenial. A refugee girl (also named Lotte, like her mistress) did most of the cooking and washing up, but the family helped with the housework.

Those first five or six days were so busy and novel for us that we hardly thought of the war. Someone told us of a cot available in a village some four miles away. Two nights together in that lumpy bed were enough to send us off at once. Erika, Hermann, and I set out with an "express wagon." It was an exciting expedition as the dive-bombers were following every road. Whenever we heard or saw one, we scrabbled under hedgerows or dove into the little foxholes when we found them. Fortunately there were few carts traveling our little road and no trucks. When we loaded the iron cot, we found it a most awkward cargo to balance, and the metal glinted dangerously in the sun. But we got safely back, and Dora and I both slept better from then on.

In that village and another we had to pass through, we were startled to see homemade white flags hanging out of every house. I had never thought of the mechanics of surrendering and was relieved to find you could possibly avert a bloody battle by waving white flags. It gave a storybook quality to this final phase of the war. When we got back I asked Herr Gries why we didn't do the same. He said he would see to it in plenty of time. But next morning some of the villagers made white flags and stuck them out. We heard that night that the German divisions in Italy had surrendered.

Next came the news that Hitler was dead, and that all the Germans and Italians in Italy and Austria had surrendered. It was hard to believe that Hitler was really dead. Everyone was awed and overjoyed at the same time. There may have been some who were sorry, though I doubt it.

The next two days were spent dashing from one village to another. One was handing out a surplus of navy cloth, and I came back triumphant with four blue-striped towels and six quaint pillowcases—coarse blue-and-white checked cotton, lapped over envelope style, and tied with strong white tape—which Dora later used to make Erika her one summer dress. In Dransau the miller was emptying his mill and, until the supply gave out, each adult on the spot received a fifty-pound sack of coarse mixed meal. Later this stood between us and starvation. Our Giekauer dairy gave us each a big, round green cheese. It was too green to have much taste, but it was protein. We could hardly believe the bounty.

Now that Admiral Doenitz (Admiral Karl Doenitz, Commander-in-Chief of the *Kriegsmarine*, who was appointed by Hitler as his successor) had surrendered, there was no longer a German government. Excitement grew as we heard of the Battle of Berlin, that Hamburg and Lübeck were occupied. We believed and hoped there would be no fighting around us, but we had heard that in a few towns where there were German detachments, the soldiers were putting up a fight. I had no idea how the end would come for us, but, fortunately, as there were no soldiers in Giekau, there were no arms, except Herr Jäger's guns.

A few days later the *Burgermeister* told us that the British would probably arrive the next morning. The village was quiet when we awoke, and every house had its white flag fluttering.

I was very conscious of my unique role and though everyone had been warned to stay indoors, I had decided to meet the British Army. After a long while a boy came running from the Neuhaus Forest. "They're coming! They've left Seekrug and are just getting into Neuhaus!" Another half an hour, and we heard a great rumble. Around the corner came a line of tanks, manned by Scots. I stood on the green beside the *Burgermeister*. Slowly they clattered along the cobblestones and came to a halt.

The *Burgermeister* stepped up. The officer in charge stood up in his tank and curtly ordered Herr Greis to surrender. The *Burgermeister* produced some dozen guns, including Herr Jäger's. Then more orders were rattled off rapidly in English. The Mayor looked uncertain.

I stepped up. "Can I interpret? I am an American." The young officer's face didn't change. "Yes. Tell him to call out all the forced labor here." I translated. Herr Gries sent for about twenty-five men, mostly Balkans.

"Do any of you speak English?" asked the officer. They shook their heads. He turned to me. "Tell them to report here tomorrow morning at nine o'clock with their things. Some trucks will be here to pick them up." I told the men in German. There were a few more instructions to the *Burgermeister*, some documents were signed in the Mayor's office, and the cortege prepared to go on to Dransau.

I stepped quickly up again. "Please tell me where I can speak to someone in authority about my personal situation."

"In Lütjenburg. The Commandant has his headquarters there."

"Could I ride there with you when you go back to Lütjenburg, please. It's such a long walk."

"Certainly not, Madam, you are a civilian."

They rolled off. It had all taken less than half an hour. I had to smile at my naiveté, trying to thumb a ride with this solemn, historic procession. Jerry and Erika and Lütti and Hermann and all the other children rushed out to greet the heroine of Giekau, and Herr Gries thanked me solemnly and wiped his sweating brow. But not even Jerry thought I had averted a battle.

Herr Pastor came out to bring me into his little sitting room for a cup of tea. The Jaegers were there and Dora. He made a short prayer, and we drank a silent toast to the end of the war. No one said much. The carnage was over, but no one had had any time or energy to formulate ideas of the future. At that moment I felt further apart from them than in war. Perhaps they all felt it would have a very different shape for me. I knew that all these friends had been antagonistic to the Nazi regime; some of them had been very outspoken and had had difficulties with the authorities. But like all the Germans I knew, once the war was on, they found it hard to take defeat. And now there seemed nothing left but wreckage—total destruction, physical and moral.

* * * * * *

Many of the Germans had not foreseen Hitler's election. Its significance and his drive for power had been understood too late. Then they hadn't believed he could possibly last and were aghast when he led them into one frightful excess after the other, and finally into war. Their initial and tragic mistake had been to let him get into power.

But there were other Germans, of all classes, who saw him as a savior, a man to lead them out of the very real and desperate economic situation beginning after World War I and worsening every year. The more intelligent and thoughtful of them were thoroughly disillusioned by the fiasco of the League of Nations after the failure of Briand and Stresemann and what seemed an almost sardonic rejection of the Germans and Austrians by the Allies in the League. In spite of many fears and misgivings, Hitler's vigorous and drastic internal reforms, long overdue, had at first given hope to many people.

There was undoubtedly a good deal of anti-Semitic feeling in Germany before World War II. There was a very large Jewish population, particularly in the cities. Over the centuries, Jews had fled to Germany to escape the ever-recurring pogroms in the ghettos of Poland and Russia. Most of them had been absorbed into the population, some by marriage, and were highly respected citizens. But after the First World War, many Germans had begun to complain of a small but visible minority of Polish and German Jewish profiteers, who were making money on the nation's economic misery. These same people ignored the fact that German non-Jewish *Schiebers*—literally "those who shove in their food"— were profiteering in exactly the same way.

By the time people realized the extent of Hitler's fanaticism and the lengths to which he would go to rid Germany of the Jews, it was too late. Hitler had succeeded in brutalizing his elite troops, the S.S. and S.A., as well as many ordinary citizens who denounced innocent neighbors to show they were good Nazis, just as the Russians and Chinese were later to do. The concentration camps were full of German gentiles, imprisoned for political reasons that were considered "crimes" against the regime, and people grew afraid for themselves and their families. Taking a stand against the Jewish outrage was a dangerous risk. No one who has not lived under a Hitler can possibly understand what it was like. The Nazi government was unbelievably well organized, for Germans are thorough and methodical by nature. There was a courageous underground, larger than people in the West realize, but there were informers everywhere and its members were wiped out time and again.

As an American, I was very cautious, but I was also lucky in spending most of my time in the country, where vigilance was not so intense and where there was usually only one Party Member in the vicinity. The extermination of the Jews was carried out so secretly that I am convinced very few knew of it until later. That many Jews had been imprisoned or shot, yes, but that the government was committing genocide and by the most hideous means, no.[13] This is not an apology for the Germans nor a justification. Germans I know have, and rightly, a sense of guilt about the Jews that will burden them as long as they live.

* * * * * *

The night of our surrender everyone made a ceremony of tearing the black-out curtains off the windows and lighting our precious candle-ends with a conscious prodigality. No more bombs; now light after darkness. Dora and the children and I stood looking out our window at all the flickering candlelights in the village cottages. It was as gay and carefree as Broadway, and we went to bed thankful, com-

---

[13] In retrospect, it's easy to forget how few people around the world actually knew what the Germans were doing in the concentration camps. Author William Shirer, in his masterful book, *The Rise and Fall of the Third Reich*, wrote: "I myself was to experience how easily one is taken in by a lying and censored press and radio in a totalitarian state. Though unlike most Germans I had daily access to foreign newspapers, especially those of London, Paris and Zurich, which arrived the day after publication, and though I listened regularly to the BBC and other foreign broadcasts....a steady diet over the years of falsifications and distortions made a certain impression on one's mind and often misled it. No one who has not lived for years in a totalitarian land can possibly conceive how difficult it is to escape the dread consequences of a regime's calculated and incessant propaganda." (Shirer, pp. 247-48)

pletely relaxed for the first time in six years.

The next morning I awoke refreshed and cheerful. I would go to see the British Commandant at Lütjenburg. It was a long, warm walk but I didn't mind. Peace in the air, hardly a cart on the road, I saw the Commandant without difficulty. He was aloof, impersonal, but listened with courtesy to my story. I asked him to send letters to the United States for me. "Madam, you must realize you are in the British Zone, not the American. Furthermore, this is a military government. We have no jurisdiction over foreign civilians here."

"But surely you can send one letter for me to the American Military Government to forward?"

"No, Madam, I cannot. You must wait until an American Consulate opens."

"When will that be?"

He shrugged. "Perhaps in two months, perhaps in two years. I do not know."

"Then," I asked, "I must go to the American Zone!"

"To us you are a German civilian, Madam, and German civilians may not travel." He paused. "I will take your name and address, and that is all I can do for you."

The interview was over. I walked back much subdued but luckily got a ride in a cart part way. And that was that.

I got home to find that all that day weary and disheveled German prisoners had limped into Giekau in twos and threes. The villagers took pity on them and squeezed the sick into corners and barns, feeding and caring for them as best they could. Twelve men appeared together at the *Pastorat*. They looked so exhausted and yet so cheerful that Frau Pastorat, in a spontaneous burst of pity, allowed them to occupy the big living-and-parish room. The family of four already there had to double up in the attic. The Twelve Apostles, as Lotte called them, took over on condition that they would sweep and air their room daily. They were a mixed dozen from all over. We became particularly attached to the mechanic from Leipzig, the bass from the Berlin Opera, and the locomotive driver from Westfalen.

We all imagined it as a very temporary arrangement, but next day more soldiers came in straggling columns, gaunt, dirty, many ill and slightly wounded. They wandered around, camping in fields and in the woods along Salenter See. And this was only the vanguard. There was grave consternation. Who was going to feed them?

> *No traveling at all*
> *No locomotion*
> *No go by land or ocean.*
> *No news, no post,*
> *No word from any foreign coast.*
> —Thomas Hood

We were in chaos. The German Government was gone. The British Military were busy organizing themselves, their vast army of captured German soldiers, and the big cities in their zone: Kiel, Lübeck, Hamburg, Hannover. They had no time for country villages. They never stopped at Giekau and seldom came through. We were left to ourselves, for better or worse.

Our amazing food system had been swept away overnight and was not yet replaced. Meat shops and markets were closed, the butcher, the baker, and the candlestick maker. We lived off our sacks of meal, our cheese, and a few potatoes. And went to bed at sundown or in darkness. There was no electricity yet and no candles to buy.

Schleswig-Holstein is a narrow stem of land thrust north between the North Sea and the Baltic, capped like a mushroom by Denmark and her islands. A roughly diagonal line separates Schleswig, the northern half, flat and marshy and facing the North Sea, from Holstein, which lies in the southeast on the Baltic, rolling, wooded, and fertile. The British drew two small half-circles of about fifteen miles or so in diameter in the middle of each coastline. Into these they were now pouring all their war prisoners, thousands of them. We called these the Black Zones. As there were no barracks in which to put the soldiers, they were quartered in the countryside, later to be sifted, screened, and finally disposed of. The prisoners could not leave the Zones, nor the civilians who lived there. By sheer bad luck we happened to be in one of them.

All over Germany all communication had ceased: no mail service, no telephone, telegraph, no radio, no newspapers. There were no trains or buses, no transportation over the whole country. And we were doubly cut off in the Black Zone.

Dora and I were now forced to take stock. We were no longer "invited out to dinner." Our most serious problem was potatoes and wood. Without them we could not survive. As the last refugees to come to Giekau, our situation was most unfavorable. Everyone else had heaps of potatoes and neat stacks of wood in the Harms' cellar. Ours, alas, were in Waren.

Herr Jäger solved the wood problem for us promptly. Though he and the Neuhaus Forest were now under the British, and no game was to be shot or wood to be cut except for them, he secretly felled some green saplings but had no time to haul them back for us. The six of us spent several days getting the logs together and dragging them home, branches, leaves, and all. We looked like Burnham Wood moving on Dunsinane. It was much harder and heavier work than I had imagined. It took us hours to cover the mile and a half, and we were completely exhausted at the end of each trip. We dumped the wood in one corner of the front lawn in complete disorder, and Hermann and Lütti hacked away at it daily.

Through Frau Harms and Herr Gries we got a few pounds of potatoes, pitifully few for our needs. There were none left to buy in the vicinity, and practically no winter carrots left over. April and May were starvation months after the long winter. So Dora and I set out every day to scour the countryside, separately, begging a few tubers here and there from reluctant farmers' wives. The land had already been scourged, and the farmers were fearful of famine, with the harvest still far off and all the soldiers hungry.

We forced ourselves to some semblance of a system. Up early to start our fire in the kitchen stove before little Lotte, the maid, started hers. When the water boiled in our cookpot, one of us threw in a handful of meal with a pinch of salt. That was our breakfast. Then we did all our chores, made the beds, swept our room and the long corridor, filled our pails of water at the pump. Then Dora and I went begging in the near neighborhood. Our dinner was usually four to six potatoes and a carrot boiled lightly, and no fat.

Frau Harms gave each of our children a raw carrot daily out of her last winter's store in her sand cellar. We'd eat meal soup again for supper. It was a starvation diet, and we were hungry all the time. Of course the children got the larger share, but we all began to feel weak and tired. Malnutrition sores broke out again on all the children, and we feared an epidemic of some kind. Actually I had no hunger pains, but we were always light-headed, as if we were living on cocktails alone. Gradually we began to feel irresponsible, all of us, and it was only our fear of starvation that drove us out to forage for food.

Our forays took us along pleasant paths. The *Bauernhofs* (farms) we stopped at were very handsome. Great solid structures, some very old, both barns and houses were of rough, small, dark-red brick, mellowed with age. The barns were massive, as large as those in Iowa, and sometimes they were joined by an ell to the houses, as in New England, to save plowing through the snow in winter. Their beauty was in their doorways, patterned arches with an overhanging roof. The interiors were clean and ordered and sweet smelling—of fresh milk, fresh hay, horses, and harnesses. There was always a dovecote, and always a big linden tree spreading fragrance and shade in the *Hof,* or a great chestnut with its "candles lighted for spring" with creamy white flowers.

But it was a grim time, and the worst of it was that we hadn't the slightest idea how long it would last. The British told us nothing.

Dora and I became aggressive and belligerent toward all who thwarted us in our quest for food. We became sly and cunning. We became worse. We even shocked ourselves. One day when we were both alone in the kitchen, we looked at the seven miserable potatoes I had just washed. Without a word, only the merest gesture to each other, Dora disappeared quickly down the cellar steps while I went to the half-open door into the corridor and stood guard. She brought up two handsome specimens in her apron and popped them into our pot.

Back in our room, later, we looked at each other star-tled, recognizing ourselves as the thieves we were. But we continued, becoming more reckless as time went on, steal-ing as many as six at a time, from different piles of course. One morning, Little Lotte impudently lifted the lid from our pot and looked slyly at us. "I didn't know you had any red potatoes!"

"Oh yes," Dora answered nonchalantly, "we have a few." And she named a certain farmer. We had actually no reds or yellows either. I got a lecture on potatoes from Dora later. I was innocently unaware that so many varieties existed, and that all country people recognized them instantly by size or shape or color, even in the pot. We were much more wary after this, but from then on we had an uneasy armed truce with Little Lotte.

We were on a desert island, swarming with bewildered men, women, and children, nearly all strangers to each oth-er. Our immediate past was fortunately obliterated, pushed back into our subconscious. The pre-war past was unreal, blurred and shadowy. The future was an absolute blank.

Few of the women knew where their husbands, rela-tives and friends were, or if they were alive. Many had been bombed out of their homes, some many times, before finally fleeing to Giekau. Their families had scattered, but where? Our men at the front, if alive, were now captured, but where and by whom? The men were also in complete darkness. They assumed their families had fled, but where? This, of course, we learned from the P.O.W.s at Giekau. Even before the field post had ceased months ago, no soldier had known where to write.

For a few days, in the midst of all these strange faces,

Dora and I felt lost and fretful. We felt more like unwanted *Flüchtlinge* than ever before in this flotsam and jetsam of people. But suddenly in the midst of the hopelessness, a strange sea-change took place, due partly to Frau Pastorat, and partly to the soldiers.

One warm evening with the northern sky still light, the piano was brought out by the Twelve Apostles and set up on the lawn. A soldier began to play popular songs like "Lili Marlene." In a few moments everyone was there, all singing lustily. We sang ballads and folk songs, hymns and old marching songs from the Middle Ages. Almost all Germans can sing, and the men are used to singing in little local choral societies and in the army. This was good music. Different men took over the piano and a fiddle appeared.

The next night we continued, only now we had a guitar, another violin, some recorders, and several lutes. Our Berlin bass sang some operatic airs. Night after night this went on, more and more talent emerged, and later and later was the piano finally taken in. We sent the children off to bed absent-mindedly, but the volume of sound filled the *Pastorat* and indeed the whole summer night. P.O.W.s from the whole area came. There were sometimes nearly two hundred of us. It was an immense release to everyone, especially the soldiers.

About two weeks after the surrender, some P.O.W. units arrived with their officers. They were under orders from the British to organize the prisoners in our area. They commandeered all barns, available or not, the lake shore, orchards and lawns, and set up one mess unit on our front lawn. Basic rations were now issued daily: the usual dark bread, a little margarine or cheese, and cabbage or potato soup, and every few days some tinned meat like Spam. This was a great relief to us all. But the Harmses were horrified to learn that not only was the mess unit on their lawn, but sixty men were to be quartered permanently on their premises: lawn, orchard, and in the hayloft.

Our rations began again. At last we knew where we were with our food. Though it was only a little more than two weeks since the war had ended in Giekau, so much had happened that it seemed much longer. We were shaking down. All who were destined to be tossed up on our island were here, *Flüchtlinge* and soldiers. We had to live together and make the best of it. It was the most crowded summer I can ever remember, crowded in space and in time. We were so busy and we accomplished so little. We were constantly tripping over each other. And no one was ever alone.

Our rations under the British were meager, about one-third of those we had received during our stay in Waren, but they were regular, and we could plan. We got very little meat or fat. Once a week one of us walked into Lütjenburg for our small ration of meat, about a pound for the six of us. Usually we got a piece of stew meat and a piece of hard sausage, occasionally a bit of salt pork.

Our breakfasts were meal soup as usual, but now each child got a large slice of bread with a thin coating of margarine, and Dora and I each half a slice. The meat made stew for two dinners; one day with a couple of leeks and carrots, the next with potatoes. It was thickened with our bit of precious *Gries*. But young radishes and carrots and greens were coming along now, and Lotte Harms gave us what she could, not much, for she was supplying many other people besides her own family. Of course, we picked dandelion greens, if any were left by the soldiers. The Giekauer dairy was now open again, and every other day the children fetched home a quart of buttermilk, which helped us enormously. (We got no sweet milk.) Then Dora had a bright idea. Why not stretch it into buttermilk soup? It became our supper every night. We stirred and stirred to keep it from burning, and blended it at the last moment with a tablespoon of our sugar-beet syrup we had hoarded between us. It was an acquired taste, exotic like olives or caviar, but it gave us a substantial meal supplemented with two slices of bread with cheese, or bread with a slice of sausage.

Our morale was now rising: the evening singing, the buttermilk soup, and most of all Frau Pastorat's morning salon.

Lotte and Fejor had an old family custom that was both exasperating and endearing. Like all true Northern people, they depended on tea, and one way or another they nearly always managed to have a few ounces in reserve. Promptly at ten o'clock every morning the kettle was put on to boil, then Herr and Frau Pastor had a dish of tea together. In happier times neighbors and friends had dropped in. Dora and I had been invited in once or twice, and it had been a welcome break. But now Lotte sorted out the sheep from the goats among the soldiers and invited several daily, as well as Dora and me. One of the children would summon us, "Frau Jentsch, Frau Lilienthal, *Sie sollen im Vati's Zimmer Tee trinken.*" ("Mrs. Jentsch, Mrs. Lilienthal, you are to come and have tea in Daddy's room.")

If we were around, we always dropped everything, washed our hands and smoothed our hair and shed our ugly aprons, and appeared as ladies. Lotte gradually sifted the soldiers down to four or five she liked best, and two or three came alternately. They were all interesting and/or attractive men. There were two Walters, who had become friends.

Walter Haake, handsome, ascetic and intense, was said to be the best organist in Germany, playing regularly in one of the old cathedral cities. Walter Henkel, somewhat younger, was a printer and painter. There was a sergeant from the Tirol, Egon Tchernikel, bluff and hearty and humorous. He was known to us all as "Onkel Egon." Then there was Lt. Pohf Weber from one of the old Hamburg shipping families, attractive, well-read, and serious, though also fun; then another painter, an interesting drama critic, from the Frankfurter Zeitung, I think, and the Herr Hauptmann (Captain) from Wien. This stalwart Viennese captain was strikingly attractive, rather like the Duke of Edinburgh with his dash and virility. He was also musical.

In this brief three-quarters of an hour, we were all taken out of ourselves. At first we felt awkward and self-conscious, for it had been so long since we had had any real adult conversation, especially between the sexes. But as the hot tea rose to our heads like several martinis, we began to relax and soon were launched into what seemed brilliant discussions of music, art, and literature. We didn't once mention food, war, or absent families.

Lotte was very musical, and both she and Fejor had read a great deal. She liked poetry and knew a good deal about painting. Dora was amusing and original, and I represented English Literature, fluently but without benefit of grammar. Herr Harms had a philosophical mind with a nice wit, and the personalities of the men began to emerge as we sipped our one cup of tea. It was an odd little salon on our desert island. We always left exhilarated, and our chores seemed a little less dull.

Although our meals filled us temporarily, fat, protein, and sugar were so obviously lacking that we were always hungry in a short time. So we decided to take in boarders. This wasn't as crazy as it sounds. The soldiers got a little margarine once a day for their bread and a can of meat twice a week. We sounded out Onkel Egon and Rolf Weber. They were delighted to turn over their meat, margarine, and *Kunsthonig* rations to us in return for a well-cooked, mid-day dinner, eaten from a table with good company. We did it for the children and shamelessly gave them the lion's share.

Our boarders also brought us bits of hoarded soap or a few cigarettes. The latter we traded for other scraps: a candle-end, good string for shoe laces, anything. We also took in washing from a few selected men, the cleanest looking. We washed and mended ragged shirts, socks, and under-wear. For this we received other odd bits, needle and thread, pins, or whatever they had or could get their hands on. Best of all was repair work. A former cobbler mended our shoes without any proper materials or tools; after a fashion he re-paired my worn briefcase and suitcases with cardboard and bits of leather and thread. Some even brought us a few car-rots or a lettuce they had come by, no questions asked. It worked out very well, and we kept our boarders for about two months.

The quartermaster and his mess units quartered on the *Pastorat* grounds were unpopular with us all from the start. The Harmses, especially Lotte, resented his being there at all and grew more indignant as time went on; and he be-came more and more like the camel in the Arab's tent. He stopped at nothing. It was more convenient for him to use our kitchen pump, and he soon began to sneak in the back door early in the morning to get water. Lotte was outraged and told him off in no uncertain terms. But he was brash and kept encroaching on our private domain, and so the feud continued, flaring up dramatically at intervals. His most serious breach of faith was to allow his men to use the family's and refugees' privies. Lotte was naturally furious. So she told him that he had to take over and keep them all emptied and spotlessly clean. This he did at first, but then lapsed badly. One day at noon, when we were all back from our various chores and errands, we saw Frau Pastorat stride through the orchard and onto the front lawn, in filthy high rubber boots and old pants, her hair tied up in an old scarf and rubber gloves on her hands.

"I wish to speak to your colonel. Call him at once." He came. "Herr Krammer, I have just cleaned out my family's privies. A disgusting job; I shall report you to headquarters if I have the slightest trouble with you from now on."

She didn't wait for an answer but swept back to the stable pump to scrub herself from head to foot. There was no more trouble with the *Oberst* (Colonel).

It was probably inevitable, given the sixty-odd people using those six privies, that every last one of us living in and around the *Pastorat* got dysentery, not only once, but over and over again all summer. (Most of the soldiers used the latrines dug in various fields.) It was hopeless, for we couldn't cure the cause, and we had no remedies, neither medicines nor proper food. Every so often, for a very persistent case, someone magnanimously forked out a little tea. Lotte gave us some, or one of our soldier friends bartered a few leaves. But every night harassed wraiths would drift noiselessly through the orchard and back through the dew, in rain or moonshine. We six were fortunate that we could go directly out our French door, but the others had to scurry up and down from the second floor or the attic. After a few weeks the worst was over for us, but it never entirely died out, sapping our strength. The soldiers, however, kept the privies very clean.

It was June 5, Herr Pastor's birthday. We had been in Giekau not quite six weeks—a lifetime, but one-dimensional, only the present. We had always lived here and had never known other places or other people.

Not only was the birthday celebration the social climax of the summer, it was a spontaneous outburst of gratitude and affection for Fejor, Lotte, and their family. No one can know what their generous hospitality, sympathy, and understanding had meant to all of us war waifs, men, women, and children. We prepared for it for days, washing and ironing our best rags, concocting poems and songs, feverishly trading some valuable scrap of soap or an old cigarette to some soldier who went far afield to find someone who had a bit of tea. I think we finally presented Herr Pastor with half a pound of mixed teas in varying stages of dryness. If you like your drinks "sec" this was it.

During the morning old friends and neighbors and parishioners from all over the big parish drove or walked to the *Pastorat* to wish him well. Both he and Lotte were wellloved. A birthday is not taken lightly in Germany, at any age. And this was the first birthday of note to be celebrated since the end of the war. Even the *Burgermeister* and his wife made a ceremonial visit.

Lotte had invited the Jägers, a few old friends, the inmates of the *Pastorat*, and some special soldier friends to come in after supper. That was the signal for Walter Haake and Walter Henkel to organize a glittering but heart-felt program for the occasion. We all trooped in to greet the Birthday Child, and then across the hall to the abode of the Twelve Apostles, swept and garnished by them. I wore my summer best, my black silk charity skirt (from Waren) and a white silk blouse. Erika was proudly decked in the blue and white checked dress Dora had made her from the pillowcases. Our boys were scrubbed and clean. The elastic on our girdles and garters had long given out and, as we no longer had any decent stockings, we went bare legged. But our old brown oxfords were clean and shining.

Everyone was given a square of simple but delicious *Streusselkuchen*, and each adult a glass of wine for the birthday toast. It went to our heads very quickly.

Then the program began. Haake and Henkel had even had a mimeographed booklet made for each of us. All talent (and it was no mean array) had been mustered. There were short speeches, original songs, and poems. Even I made some doggerel which was much applauded, a wonderful mixture of German and English: *"Bei die Pumpe in der Küche der Oberst putzen sein Stieffel und die Frauke putzen ihre Zahn"* (By the pump in the kitchen, where the Colonel polishes his boots, and Frauke polishes her tooth), but it all rhymed! Several real musicians had composed special music, the bass from the Berlin Opera sang his heart out magnificently in several numbers, and then we had our usual repertoire of old favorites, polished for the occasion. Onkel Egon gave his specialty, always much appreciated, the dolorous ballad of the Ritter Hadubrand, which brought down the house. Walter Haake, with great feeling, sang a tragic song of a pig, in Latin. And there was a poem set to music for Little Lotte, the maid, for it was her birthday too.

Then came our favorite communal ballad which we all sang with gusto, a long, repetitive affair about the Butter Robber of Halbrstadt, and last our Giekauer themesong, *"Caramba."* This is a short but rousing ballad about *"Don*

Alfonso, hoch zu Ross (O caramba) Ging auf Abenteuer los (O caramba)" etc. (Don Alfonso high on his white horse went to seek adventure.) The chorus of each verse was shouted as fast as possible:

> "O caramba, o caramba,
> Rio de Janeiro Montevideo!"

We gave it its full due that evening.

There was one small contretemps, which added merriment. Frau Pastorat's nannygoat sauntered into the parlor to wish Herr Pastor a happy birthday before the other guests had arrived and ate up all the roses. This entertained everyone except Herr Haake. It was a party to be remembered, gay and heart-warming. At least in one spot in Germany, the natives, the *Flüchtlinge* and the P.O.W.s were united in goodwill, and this never really deteriorated afterwards.

Though we were still obsessed with finding more food for our children, I had noticed that each mother had for some time relaxed her maternal responsibility and vigilance. The children did their chores, but they roamed the countryside free and untrammeled. We had been forced to such relentless vigilance during the war and had kept such close hold on them, that now mothers and children seemed to drift apart and go their separate ways in Giekau. All the children went barefoot. Ours had only their heavy ski boots left now. And they were very good, never asking for more bread or complaining of hunger. We were not starving, but it was a marginal existence. Our stomachs had certainly shrunk, but there were no colds, no bilious upsets, only dysentery and the constant sores that wouldn't heal.

Hermann, I know, was bored a good deal of the time.

He went around with the few older boys but found no one very congenial. He and Erika foraged everywhere for books and read everything they could lay their hands on. He entertained Jerry by the hour when he was bored, drawing pictures for him of "Cayman" and East Prussia, cars, and planes and battle scenes; and what entertained me most, idyllic scenes of American life, full of the most remarkable mechanical gadgets and luxuries. He also had a special soldier friend, as did most of the children. He and I also had a special affinity. He often went with me on my foraging walks, and we spoke English together. An unusually handsome boy, he had a sensitive imagination and an interesting mind. He was very curious about America and asked me endless questions.

Jerry played mainly with Jochen Jäger and the other small boys. Lütti (Ernst) was a most engaging urchin. He and Erika were the best of friends, both lively and adventurous. He had a gang of boys, native and *Flüchtlinge*, and Erika was the only girl allowed in it. She told me later that they let her in mainly because of her boy's corduroy knickerbockers from Waren, of which she was very proud. But she was much more of a tomboy than the other girls. They roved the fields and woods and took part in periodic gang wars with the Dransau boys. But she also played with the other girls, especially Waldtraut Jäger.

Erika and Lütti had many an adventure together. There was one particular expedition that they both like to remember. We heard of a cobbler plying his trade in a distant village, and our shoes were all in great need of repair. Lütti and Erika started early one morning into unknown territory, northeast toward the Baltic. All our heavy boots were thrust into their rucksacks, with a picnic lunch of bread and cheese and carrots, and they danced off barefoot down the road and over the hills. On their way, they visited Ernie, their particular soldier friend now quartered in a far village. Then, over the hill the shimmering blue sea had suddenly burst upon them, stretching to the far horizon. They came back at the end of the day, still dancing. They had covered many miles, over dunes and moorland, and seen many strange sights!

In spite of being always hungry, the children had a wonderful summer. It was such pretty country and they knew every stick and stone in it. They had wild games of "I Spy" and "Prisoners Base" in the dark, and I introduced our old Louisville favorite of "How Many Miles to Barley Bright?" which was the most exciting of all. Or so I thought, until years later Erika told me of their visits to the Crypt in the dead of the night. Someone knew where the key hung, and the more daring and ghost-minded children crept down into the dark dankness to tell ghost stories. The great attraction was some ancient bones lying loose in the corner!

There were some real ogres in Giekau, too. Behind the *Pastorat*, separated by a lane and a stone wall, was a *Bauern* belonging to Farmer Kobalt. (*Kobalt* means a kind of goblin in old Germanic and Norse.) He was a surly misogynist and especially detested children and refugees. So naturally it was the children's delight and terror to scramble over his wall for apples and other pleasures. Not only was there Bauer Kobalt to encounter, but *Dogge* Kobalt, the fierce mastiff chained to a tree in the *Hof*, who often got loose. Best of all was *Bulle* Kobalt in a little pasture perilously near the churchyard wall. He, also, sometimes got loose. This was a most formidable trio and a delightful challenge.

Naturally it was forbidden to enter the Kobalt realm, but

who could resist? There were many repercussions, but no really disastrous results. These animals were somehow very individual and significant, called by their master's felicitous patronymic, and seemed to come quite naturally by their fierceness. It was always "Bulle Kobalt," and "Dogge Kobalt" and "Bauer Kobalt," just like "Puppe Pastor" in Pommern.

In a strange way, not only the children but the adults enjoyed life. Our world was so tiny and yet so full, and there was always something of interest going on. We had none of the larger, more complex, issues of life—just the simple problem of getting enough to eat. We had no future at the moment, so we didn't try to grapple with its problems. Dora and I often sat in the warm sun on our doorstep doing our mending, while the bees droned round us in the orchard and clover. Frauke or Lotte would stop by for a chat, or one of our soldiers, waiting for his socks to be darned. Sometimes we had a more sinister occupation, grimly examining each other's heads for lice. I combed poor Erika's long hair daily, searching her scalp minutely for nits. We did our weekly wash at the pump in the backyard near the orchard, each woman having her turn at the two tin washtubs, and this was also a social occasion.

The big cheerful kitchen was the center of our communal life. Besides the Harmses and us, another family cooked here, Frau Rix and her little boy. (Two kitchens had been improvised upstairs to take care of the rest.) But everyone had to pass through our kitchen at least twice a day to get their stores in the cellar and draw their water from the pump. It was the clearinghouse for gossip, complaints and grievances, jokes, quarrels, and exchange of rumors. We washed ourselves in our own rooms, but the Harms boys who lived in the big larder, had to wash in the kitchen, and gradually Frau Harms' pet soldiers who lived on the place began to shave there and clean their boots. I shudder now when I think of the *Pastorat* hygiene. When we had a salad or anything that couldn't be dumped into our stew or soup, Frau Rix and Dora and I had to snatch the enamel basin in the sink used by everyone for washing their hands. And as soap was extremely scarce and all our hot water had to be heated in the great teakettle, no one wasted much of either. Sometimes we saved soapy water for several days and then re-heated it!

On Saturday nights the Harmses, the Lilienthals, the Rixes, and the Jentschs all had baths there, one after another, in two tin washtubs on the floor. It was the only spot in the house warm enough, and it was too arduous to carry the tubs around and fill them. It was a very lively scene, what with the whistling and singing and shouting, scolding and laughing, and general confusion. When the last child had emerged from the steam, like a red lobster from the pot, been rubbed down and scrambled into a nightgown and shot out the door to bed, we women had to mop up and put the kitchen straight. It was fun—once a week.

Onkel Egon taught the children to swim in the lake, and sometimes Dora and I and the other women and girls went in, but as there were only three bathing suits in the *Pastorat*, we couldn't all go at once. Whenever we went, some fifty soldiers had to be alerted so they could put on their underpants.

Every so often we tried to organize school for the children. Many soldiers offered to teach them, but it generally degenerated into a swimming lesson or a game of tag. One man who said he had been a teacher had a class of about six, including Lütti and Erika and Jerry. It turned out that he was obsessed with etiquette and had the children sneak cups and saucers and silverware from the *Pastorat* to teach them table manners on a stone slab in the churchyard. I was soon petitioned to give English lessons, which I did daily, also in the graveyard, to some twenty soldiers. My fame grew, and some P.O.W. officers billeted two villages away came and picked me up in a truck once a week to teach them for two hours. They paid with cigarettes and money, and once or twice we had a cup of real coffee at the end of the lesson.

One day I was summoned to Gottesgabe to teach the owners. Twice a week I walked there and was driven back (the farm horses couldn't be spared for the two trips, they said). It was about three and a half miles, past Neuhaus and down the dirt road to the main Lütjenburg road, which I crossed at Seekrug, and then on west to Gottesgabe. It was a very handsome old estate, almost as busy as the Heckers'. I found we were only going to have conversation, but I thought it odd that I conversed with the lady of the house first and her husband later. She was pretty and pleasant, but seemed unhappy. Her husband had been badly lamed early in the war and sent back to run the estate. At the end of the two hours we all three had tea together, and I left in a trap with great satisfaction and a string bag full of vegetables and a sausage.

When I got home Frau Pastorat said, "Look out for him, he's something of a rake." After the second lesson, his wife didn't appear, and he offered me *Schnaps*, which I regretfully refused. As I was starting out the next time, Dora called out to me that I was selling my soul for a cabbage, but to keep on just the same, as we needed the cabbage. Lotte was right, and I stopped going after the fifth time.

We still sang on the lawn several times a week, and now someone suggested a dance. A dance! As far as I knew there wasn't a dissenting voice in the *Pastorat*. All the furniture was hauled out of the Apostles' room, and everyone contributed candle stubs. (There was now about two hours of electricity a night, usually between eight and ten.)

We were a freakish looking lot to be gathered for a ball with no lipstick, no stockings, no slippers, but at least we were clean and neat, even the soldiers. It was a curious affair, almost too gay and spirited. Later it began to take a macabre turn. First one man and then a second, who had been gay and flirtatious, abruptly left their partners in the middle of a waltz and disappeared. They had been overcome by sudden thoughts of wives who were God knew where, if still alive. It was too sudden, and we were not prepared for a dance and all the associations it might bring. Nevertheless, it was pronounced a great success. The children watching from outside and at the top of the steps were completely entranced. For them "all the beauty and the chivalry of the Belgian capitol were gathered there that night." Erika was absolutely dazzled by the brilliant scene.

But it had its inevitable consequences. The northern summer had already transformed the countryside, and now it began to work its perverse magic on us. As the summer nights grew warmer and longer, our desert island bloomed into romance. Soon pairs of lovers were strolling about in the dusk and on into the moonlight. Most of the romances were just flirtations of the shipboard type, stemming from boredom and proximity. But some of them were real and intense. A pretty young woman from Magdeburg, who lived in the *Pastorat* upstairs with her mother, had been the most exemplary soldier's wife but was now seriously entangled with an older man.

Walter Haake had early been obviously attracted to Frau Pastorat, but she deftly steered him to Frauke. He was now passionately attached to her, and they spent hours in the church, while he taught her to play the organ. Frauke, I may say, was able to take care of herself, and I don't think she ever lost her head or her heart to Lt. Haake, but she was flattered and enjoyed the attention of such a distinguished and ardent older man.

But the love affair of the summer was that of the Herr Hauptmann von Wien and the Frau Pastorat. It was at the same time the most flagrant and the most innocent. Dora and I both knew that Lotte and our handsome Captain from Vienna had become very good friends, but we were astounded to see now that they had fallen deeply in love. He was a few years younger, but it didn't seem to matter. They were completely open about it. They couldn't help it, they couldn't hide it, and there it was, for all to see. It was as if they didn't see the rest of us.

Herr Pastor gave no indication to us, except that he was quieter. The lovers had much in common, especially music. He had an excellent tenor and Lotte a sweet contralto. You'd find them singing duets anywhere at any time, when she should have been attending to a hundred duties. In the orchard, under the big linden tree, in the churchyard, and often at night we'd hear the two of them in the kitchen next to our room, sitting on the big round table, singing softly long past midnight.

The summer wore on, and a general feeling of restiveness grew. Still no communication or contact with the outside world, not even the military authorities. The soldiers, in particular, had nothing to do. Some of them had picked up jobs with the farmers, but the great mass of them wandered aimlessly around. There were no materials or tools to ply any trade. Some borrowed books from the natives and read or studied. Many helped the women with their heavier work. Some carved little things out of wood. Some argued and fought. All of them went in the lake swimming, washing themselves and their clothes at the same time. It was very demoralizing for them, and I am surprised that nothing serious happened.

We women were very busy. We were as busy as ants gathering food, but unlike them, we didn't really believe in our activity. We couldn't find enough food, nor the right kind. It kept us alive, but we had no strength or resistance.

It was almost two months since the war's end and still "no post, no word from any foreign coast." There were only rumors. In Lütjenburg we tried to find out what was happening but the British were not talking, at least to us in the Black Zone. We only knew that the far eastern provinces—Silesia, Pomerania, Mark Brandenburg (between Pommern and Silesia) and East Prussia—had been given to Poland and Russia, and that half the rest of Germany was in the Russian Zone, now East Germany, including Mecklenburg almost as far west as Lübeck.

The big church was crowded every Sunday, and Herr Pastor preached some good sermons, some stern, some comforting, but a state of tension had set in. As far as we knew, there was still no organization for German *Flüchtlinge*, no place to find out where families were, and no place to write to give our address even if the post office had been functioning.

One night a young woman from East Prussia disappeared from Giekau, leaving a note for Herr Pastor. She had gone to try and find her only child, lost somewhere in Mecklenburg. She had been half-crazed, they said, when she arrived, but later had had an affair with a soldier. Now she could stand it no longer and had fled to the Russian Zone. A few days later, another mother left her two children in the care of a farmer's wife and went back into the imprisoned East to search for her oldest child, a boy of seven. How they got through the barriers, and what happened to them, we never knew. They were never heard of again. This increased the tension in Giekau.

On Midsummer's Eve, we awoke to great activity. Soldiers and boys were seen carrying great armfuls of brushwood from Neuhaus Forest. At sundown there was a tremendous pile on our front lawn. We hastily got through our chores and ate our supper in a state of excitement. Everyone belonging to the *Pastorat* was there, and then came others from the village—P.O.W.s, women, and children— until the lawn was filled with expectant people. *Walpurgis* Night!

We all went pagan as the great fire began to crackle and roar, silhouetting dramatically the old church tower. We sang, a hundred voices swelling and rising with the flames, until the great blaze finally died down to a molten mass of brightly glowing embers. Frauke Harms was one of the first to leap across it, with Walter Haake behind her, then the soldiers and boys and everyone else who dared. We lost all sense of time and forgot ourselves completely. It is hard to imagine now, but we were under a spell, in the shadow of the church. Finally we came to. The fire was put out, the children hustled off, and we all went to bed to sleep soundly, curiously released from our tensions.

A Midsummer's Eve to remember. It had acted as a purge to us. From then on we were more normal, and a sense of responsibility returned to most of those who had lost it. Many of the flirtations petered out.

But the affair of Lotte and the Hauptmann had burst into full flower. Lotte was as one bewitched. Day after day she abandoned all domestic duties except her vegetable garden, in which she worked like mad, the Captain helping her. We felt very sorry for Herr Pastor but could understand how it happened. Though they were congenial companions and she was obviously very fond of him, she was so much younger. Perhaps she had never really been in love before. And while she seemed normally devoted to her children and conscientious, Lotte wasn't primarily a mother. Whatever the reasons, it was obviously a grand passion.

Day after day, the two lovers set out in her little rowboat on the big lake, picnicking in some cove and returning only at sunset. Frauke was heard to complain wryly one day that Mutti had used up all the family sugar for the boat teas. Now we knew that she was in extremis. In our time and situation, for a mother to take food from her children indicated practically a crime *passionelle*.

The Jägers said very little to us, but they were truly horrified, and so were many old friends of the Harmses in the country around. First the evening singing, then the dance—two black marks against Frau Pastorat in the Black Book of the Parish—then a third, more serious—our "pagan rites" of Midsummer's Eve—and now the fourth, the most flagrant of all, which could not be overlooked by the church elders and many of the parishioners, no matter how devoted they were to both the Harmses. Herr Pastor Harms was relieved of his parish some months after I left. But the *Flüchtlinge* and the P.O.W.s will always remember Lotte and Fejor with warmth and gratitude. Those first three items in the Black

Book did much to help our morale.

The summer wore on. The farmers' crops ripened, and it was harvest time. The edict came through from Preetz, our rationing center, that after the harvest we refugee women and children could glean. This meant potatoes and beans. We streamed barefoot out to the potato fields first, with sacks, baskets, and aprons, to pick up what was left. Rarely did we find a real potato; most of them were the hard little green fruit, considered inedible, and, I think, poisonous to cattle. But we put them in our aprons and the six of us brought back perhaps a meager basketful, real and green together. We came out better with the beans, but it was back-breaking work. After us, the soldiers swarmed over the fields.

Onions were very scarce, and we could neither beg not steal any, but we did get some leeks from Lotte and the farmers, and they were highly prized. Leek and potato soup is a delectable dish, practically *Vichyssoise*. When the elderberries ripened, we took the children and stripped the bushes. Sweetened with a little of our beet syrup, we made a dessert of meal or *Gries* flavored with elderberry juice, our first real dessert. We also gathered rose hips and haws from the wild rose hedges for vitamins.

Salenter See was a favorite resting place for a great variety of sea birds. Sometimes they came by preference, but often they were blown in by the great gales that swept over us from both the Baltic and the North Sea. Herr Jäger shot a large sea fowl one day—I can't remember what it was—and gave it to Dora and me. We hung it for quite a while, but when we finally cooked it, it was too fishy to eat.

One summer's day, very early in the morning while I was still abed, a magpie darted through the open French doors, paused a moment on the bureau, and flew impudently off with a tiny shining object. My little gold pin! He never brought it back.

There is one pleasant episode in that summer that I like to remember. I was handed a note from Neuhaus one day, in excellent English and signed "Maria, Prinzessin von Sachs-Altenburg." Would I, if I had the time and energy, come over and have tea with her? I would. She also was a refugee, living in two small rooms in the *Graf's* big manor house with her little adopted son Franzi and an elderly female retainer.

I went back frequently for she had often visited royal English relatives and wanted very much to keep up the language. Her father had been at the Russian court, and she had lived most of her childhood there. At some point she had lost an eye and wore a black patch, which made her look even more beautiful and sad. I grew very fond of her. She was trying to get to relatives either in Lippe or in Bavaria, and I helped her write a letter to the British. Her ultimate dream was to go to South America, where she had one or two relatives, and start life over for herself and Franzi. She never did leave Neuhaus. She died about a year after I got back to America.

One fine morning in early July, Frau Pastorat suggested that some of us take a picnic to a *Huhner Graben,* a dolmen not far away. I hadn't known how profusely these prehistoric monuments were scattered along the Baltic and was delighted. So she and Dora and Frau Jäger and Frauke and I and several of our special soldier friends, along with our children, started off early. It was the only time I went off the beaten track, on pure pleasure bent. I never got to Kiel, nor to the Baltic. We walked along lanes bordered with hedgerows and then over rolling moors, lovely country, green and empty. In the hush of noon we entered a deep wood with sunlight filtering through the beeches. Suddenly we came upon a small clearing, and there it was. Great tall slabs of stone in a rough triangle, partially covered with moss and lichen. Clear water was trickling over one fallen giant from a hidden spring. It was very still and very ancient. Merlin's enchantment lingered on in this secret wood and even the children were quiet. We finally left to eat our lunch on a sunny hilltop, but the spell was not exorcised until we got back to Giekau. This was one of the nicest days I remember.

As the middle of August approached, subtle changes appeared. To our consternation, food was even scarcer after the harvest. It all had to be sent to the crowded cities, now that the Eastern breadbasket was lost to the Russians and Poles. Also the British Military needed some of it. But now came the first trickling of messages from lost husbands, and a few of our P.O.W.s had word from wives and mothers, all through chance messengers. Still no mail or public services except a little more electricity.

A stranger appeared one day, a demobilized soldier, the husband of a young woman who had been having a flirtation with one of our men. Our strange wonderland was being invaded by reality, and his arrival blew away many a romance. The future was moving in on us, though not yet for Dora and me. Our money was getting low, our clothes were worn out, and no message came for us from Outside.

I knew that Hamburg was the largest city in the British Zone, so there should be some American soldiers there as liaison officers. I must get to Hamburg, but how? As a civilian I couldn't cross our P.O.W. Black Zone without a permit, and these were notoriously rare. Transportation was an even more serious obstacle. Early in August I found a German quartermaster in the P.O.W. *Commissariat* in a nearby village who was being sent to Hamburg. He promised I could go south with him—if I had papers. I assured him I had. On August 5, 1945, in my old farmer's boots, a jacket borrowed from Dora, an old tweed skirt darned in vital spots, and a kerchief over my head, I set out with the quartermaster into the unknown, rucksack on my back containing a nightgown, a change of underwear, half a loaf of bread, cheese, and a piece of hard *Wurst*. Erika and Jerry, Hermann and Lütti and Dora, all waved me off with high hopes that I might return with untold riches in the way of food and shoes. The first lap to the Black Zone border was very exhilarating. I was going off in peacetime, no bombs, no fear of any kind. And I was traveling into the great world to meet my fellow countrymen. I had never been to Hamburg, though in a straight line, it is only about sixty-five miles from Giekau; in our present situation it seemed as far as Paris.

We reached the Black border and halted, along with several other vehicles, as two Tommies stood in the road. Papers? The quartermaster and a local butcher produced theirs and were duly passed. My American passport cancelled in Berlin in the winter of '43 was examined. Where are you going and why? I told my story: to find an American liaison officer in Hamburg to help me and my children return to the United States. Impassively they told me to get down and report to their colonel in the house down the road. The quartermaster was impatient. I must hurry.

I was escorted into the house and through an open door I saw the colonel asleep in a very rumpled bed. The corporal was embarrassed. He tried to wake his commanding officer, who would have none of it. Finally, "What the hell. Let her go," came through to me in thick blurred tones. I was quickly escorted back to the truck and off we went, very fast. We had left soon after daybreak and would reach our destination in good time. The countryside was smiling in the sun and seemed new and gay and excitingly strange. But as we approached the suburbs of Hamburg, everything changed. We passed through miles of chaotic rubble. There were no landmarks, just block after block of endless destruction. I had forgotten what to expect. Once in the heart of the city, there were buildings still standing, and I began to realize what a big place Hamburg was.

I climbed down from the truck stiff and dazed. I was on the Ufer, the banks of the Elbe. The streets were filled with people, some dazed and aimless like myself, obviously *Flüchtlinge*, others scurrying along, and always British soldiers walking alertly but impassively in pairs. Lean and hard and brown they looked—and very detached and aloof from the German civilians. Finally I accosted a pair, asking in English, "Please tell me where to find the Americans?"

"Americans?" They shook their heads. "This is the British Zone. There are no Americans here."

"But there must be at least some liaison officers?"

They shook their heads. They'd never seen any. I left them, momentarily deflated. Then I walked on and finally saw an American flag waving from the top of a large building which had "Hamburg-Amerika Line" on it.

Relieved, I entered a big lobby. No one there. Walking through long corridors, I finally met a man and asked him to direct me to "the Americans." He seemed surprised, then indicated stairs. I found an inhabited office at last and asked to speak to the American in charge.

A young American in civilian clothes and in a great hurry came out to me. I never knew who or what he was. He was very pleasant and sympathetic to my story. He was the only American in Hamburg, he told me, and unfortunately he had to make a plane in twenty minutes. I was unfortunate. He hurriedly advised me to go to the D.P. camp here. They'd take care of me. After giving me the address, he apologetically rushed off. I was cheered by my encounter with such a friendly and pleasant countryman, but what was a D.P. camp?

Out on the Ufer again, I made inquiries. Yes, there was a Displaced Persons Camp about an hour's walk from here. An hour's walk to a German is about a two hour's walk to anyone else. I don't remember seeing a tram. So it was after four when I finally found the camp.

I told my story, showed my papers and filled out many forms. The young woman told me that all the people in the camp were displaced persons such as I and were waiting to be transported to their homes or the U.S.A. This was exciting news. How simple it all was, and why hadn't I come before, I wondered. Then someone else told me to go to a small shack across the road while she read my forms.

There I was greeted by a girl who had barely nodded to me before she snatched off my kerchief and sprayed my head with a cloud of choking powder, then whisked up my skirt and sprayed copiously again. I was dumbfounded until she apologized and explained that it was done to everyone on entering the camp. I asked her what it was. D.D.T to kill lice. D.P. and D.D.T: I had never heard of either before. When I asked her for a little bag of this miracle powder to take back to Giekau, she was astonished in turn and gave me about a pound, which I stowed in my rucksack. We had need of it in Giekau.

Hope was running high. My troubles were about over, even to vermin. But back in the office, the girl asked me where my two children were. I explained. Well, she said, you have to have them here with you, and then you must be screened by the authorities in order to find out if you're a bona fide D.P., and only then can you become inmates of the camp. Most of these people have already been here months, and they are all from former concentration camps, or forced labor of the Germans. I asked her where to find the authorities. "Why, at British Headquarters."

It was getting late when I got back to the center of town. Where to sleep? I hadn't thought of that before. I suppose I had vaguely thought some women and girls would take me to straw and hot soup as usual. I stopped another pair of Tommies. One was very helpful and told me where to find headquarters, but it was now closed until morning.

Where could I sleep? They hadn't any idea but finally remembered that there was a temporary camp for German refugees a couple of miles away where I probably could stay. By that time I was weary and hungry, and I found that my Black Zone food cards were not valid here. It was late when I got to the barracks, a very dreary place, forlorn with broken windows and no straw, and crowded with Germans.

I asked for a place to sleep and some supper, but when I showed my passport, they said I was not a German. Why didn't I go to the D.P. Camp? I said firmly that it was too late now and I had to stay. They gave me some *malz* coffee, and I ate my bread and cheese and sat on a bench all night with several others. They were all women and children, just as it had been on our flight, only now I was alone. Also they were very disheartened, as they had been here so long and could find no place to go. I felt very much alone and lost, coming from the friendly bustle of Giekau. Early next morning, I washed my face and hands at a tap, tidied my deloused hair and left for British Headquarters. Outside I was astonished to see long queues of Germans. I joined one line and in about an hour reached the entrance. "Your permit slip?" a soldier asked me.

"Where do I get one?" The soldier pointed across the street, and around the corner.

Even longer queues there. That day was a total failure. The doors were closed over the noon period. I ate more bread and some *Wurst* on the curb and stood again in line. At the end of the afternoon I got my permit to stand in line at headquarters, but too late, of course, to go back.

And now where to sleep tonight? I would not go back to the refugee camp. It was too far and too dismal. I wandered along the streets and at last with little hope, I asked two Britishers again. Very correct and unsmiling, they said there was no place for a respectable woman to sleep and didn't I know there was a curfew for civilians at eight p.m.?

Dazed, I said no, I was a stranger here from up country. Well, I'd better find a place directly. It was now nearly 7:45. I made a show of walking away purposefully and briskly.

At two minutes past eight along came another pair of Tommies. They stopped me. I quickly and somewhat nervously told them my story briefly. They looked at each other and then at me. "I'm sorry, but we'll have to arrest you, Madam." Arrest me?

Embarrassed, they told me the facts of life. Every woman on the streets after eight was arrested as a prostitute and taken to German police headquarters. At first I sputtered in indignation.

"Then arrest me," I said. They were even more embarrassed, but we started off without a word, and they left me with obvious relief at the civilian police headquarters.

The officer in charge was a harassed but kind-looking man, and I told my story as pathetically as I could. There wasn't a bed in Hamburg for a lady, or anyone else, he said.

"Well, why can't I stay here all night?"

He looked startled, but finally said, "Why not, if you don't mind. There is no other place."

He led me into a tiny anteroom, and with a couple of kitchen chairs I settled down contentedly, munching the last of my cheese and bread. I was glad to get off my feet. I was too excited to sleep and sat out the night with the door open watching the scene.

Prostitutes were brought in, some obviously the real thing and some innocent women caught by the curfew. They were all sent elsewhere. Most of the other arrests were petty thieves—food and bicycle thieves, many of them young boys. Around one a.m. a policeman brought me a cup of coffee. A really interesting night.

Next morning a new shift came on; the elderly officer brought me a cup of weak but real coffee and a slice of bread and margarine and let me wash my face and hands. After thanking them for my entertaining night, I was on my way to British Headquarters.

I got under the rope just before noon and saw the Commandant. He listened courteously to my story. What did I want of him? I wanted first to send letters to America to my relatives and friends, especially some influential ones in the State Department. I mentioned Jake Beam and Llewellyn Thompson. I wanted to get myself and my children to

America as soon as possible, and I wanted more food for my children while we waited. Getting the letters off was the important first step, as no one knew where I was, if alive or dead.

Still courteous, but impassive, he told me that because I was an American in the British Zone, he had no jurisdiction over me; but that at present he must consider me a German civilian as my American passport was cancelled and I had not yet been screened by American consular authority. I asked him when and where this could be done. As far as he knew there was no U.S. consulate yet opened in the American enclave of Bremen in the British Zone. I told him my children were both American citizens and that I had papers to prove it. But he could do nothing for me. He was very sorry, but he could not even send one letter for me. I asked him if he couldn't write a letter himself to his American opposite number somewhere in the American Zone. He either couldn't or wouldn't. This I could never understand, but I saw it was useless to argue or plead. Go back to Holstein and wait, he told me, rising to end the interview.

In my disappointment I had forgotten to mention to him that I had no more food, could get none here, and now would have to stay another night in Hamburg and had no place to sleep. I wandered along the Ufer thinking of the people of Hamburg leaping into the water in flames from the phosphorous bombs. I realized what a proud and beautiful city Hamburg had once been.

Suddenly down a side street I saw the good old white cross on the red ground, the Swiss flag. It was the Swiss consulate, and I walked in. A very pleasant white-haired woman listened sympathetically to my woes. The Swiss Consulate was in charge of American interests, she told me. When she saw the children's Geneva birth certificates in elaborate French calligraphy, bedecked with large red seals and ribbons, she was completely won over and with tears in her eyes made out a *Schweitzer Schutzschein* (Swiss Protective Certificate). Fortunately I had an extra passport photograph of the three of us with me. This document was very vague, with mostly negative phrases such as "Bearer of the certificate does not possess Swiss nationality" and "Bearer of this certificate is not entitled to enter Switzerland." But it did state that we were nationals of the United States.

She also could not undertake to send or write a letter for me; but she shared some tea and toast and marmalade with me, which, with her friendly sympathy, cheered me up out of all proportion to the official help I had received. I was at least in the vague but safe orbit of serious, stolid Switzerland that, after all, had been my home for eleven years. As I was leaving with grateful thanks, she remembered that the International Red Cross had just opened its first German office in Lübeck and suggested that I try to get there.

Now I had an objective again. While I strolled along in the sun by the Elbe, I tried to form a plan. Finding my way to the railroad station, I learned that there was one train a day to Lübeck, but I couldn't go direct from Hamburg as the rails were still out. I would have to take a local about ten miles or so south and change at Harburg. As the train went only mornings, I would be a guest of Hamburg for one more night.

Well before 8 p.m. I put in a confident appearance at my police station. They were somewhat taken aback but rallied when I told them this was positively my last time. After a night on a more comfortable bench, on which I dozed through most of the routine of bicycle thieves and prostitutes, I had my breakfast of hot coffee and fresh bread and left them with real gratitude for their hospitality.

I reached Harburg before noon. It was not a long ride to Lübeck, and I enjoyed every minute of it. I was on a train with no fear of dive bombers and going in the direction of Holstein and home. Furthermore, I'd never seen Lübeck. Walking up from the station I saw the famous squat round towers and gates of the old Hansa capitol, just like the pictures. But inside the walls the damage was appalling. There was still enough left of some of the ancient buildings to see how beautiful they once had been. I was glad to be in a small city. I was worn out from walking back and forth across the vast distances of Hamburg, especially as it was very warm in my high boots, and the two pairs of wool socks I had to wear to keep them from chafing were sodden with sweat.

The first person I saw directed me to the newly opened International Red Cross. There were just two rooms in a small building, and only one woman in charge as far as I could see. I could send one postcard, she said, to my nearest relative and put it in the slot of the small box on the wall. I filled it out, very simple as it was intended for P.O.W.s. All I could write was my name and present address and check "Well" or "Not Well." But I was in a quandary. I knew Mother had moved to New York, but I wasn't sure of the address. So I addressed it to Jake Beam, Care of the State Department, Washington.

The Swiss woman left the room at that moment, and I snatched some ten more cards and quickly addressed them to all of my relatives and friends whose addresses I could remember and pushed them all hastily through the slot. Mission accomplished. Now I could go back home to the children and wait for those eleven cards to bear fruit.

But it was getting late. I found British Headquarters in one of the few old buildings more or less intact and was taken with no permit or red tape or waiting to a handsome, reserved young Scots officer. He listened with the usual British courtesy to my glib recital of a tale that was beginning to pall on me now. I asked him for a place to stay the night and then boldly demanded transportation back to the children.

"You say you have come from north Holstein? Just where?"

"Giekau. Giekau near Lütjenburg."

His expression was rather sardonic. "Lütjenburg. I see. In the Prisoner Zone. How did you get out?"

I blushed. I had to confess that I had no permit. Neither the corporal at the border nor I had remembered it after the embarrassing behavior of the drunken colonel, and I didn't think it politic to mention that.

"Well here you are," he said grinning, "but with no permit to re-enter the Zone." Before I could ask him to give me one, he said, "Of course, if you came over 'black' I cannot give you a re-entry permit. You'll just have to crawl back through the bars."

I was annoyed but not worried. I had no doubt of getting back. Then suddenly he said, "I can do this. Here is a chit that will get you a seat on the first bus to leave Lübeck since the end of the war. This is a reserved seat, remember, not a ticket." I was overwhelmed at this royal treatment.

"When does it leave?" I asked.

"Monday morning at 11:45."

"But this is only Saturday. I'll have to stay here two nights!"

"Oh, so you will...er...but where will you stay?" We both looked blank. "Unfortunately, Madam, we have no quarters available for Allied ladies. I'll ring up the German Chief of Police. He'll have to find you a place." He called him, saying that he was leaving in twenty minutes, and that he, the Chief of Police, must find suitable quarters for an Allied lady, and be here to escort her there at once.

The Police Chief evidently expostulated over the telephone, but the Colonel cut him short. "It's up to you. I'm leaving in fifteen minutes. You will find the lady here," and rang off. "There aren't any rooms, suitable or not, but he'll have to find something." He busied himself arranging his papers, cleaned his pipe and put it in his pocket, then stamped my billet to the bus-driver. He handed it to me with a bow. "Good luck at the border," and left just as the old Chief of Police—another kind, elderly man—came running up the stairs.

As we went down the long stone steps together, he told me apologetically that he had called up every place in town—hotels, rooming houses, private families—but like every place else in Germany there just wasn't a corner. I knew. But at last he had ordered the best hotel in town to put me somewhere. It was filled with British personnel.

"They'll find a bed somewhere. But they can't feed you," he said sadly. I told him that my food had completely run out, that I had only had coffee and bread for the last two meals and that my ration cards seemed to be no good around here. When he left me at the hotel, he divided his fresh loaf with me. The other half he had to take home.

I had a tiny maid's room with no window on the top floor. But the bed was clean, and after drinking a whole pot of malz coffee and some bread the waiter brought me in the lobby, I slept long and soundly. After a late breakfast of coffee and bread, I wandered out to see Lübeck.

I was sorry I had not seen it before the war. I sat down on a bench in a little green place near the naughty Knight Roland fountain, and a comfortable old couple offered me some of their lunch, some bread and *Wurst*. I tried not to eat more than my share, but it certainly revived me. Back at the hotel the waiter sneaked me a hard-boiled egg with my bread and coffee. Perhaps if I had bribed him I could have got more, but I didn't yet know what my hotel bill would be and there still would be bus fare. When had I last paid fare? I couldn't squander my money, though I still didn't think of it as having any value.

Monday morning there was quite a crowd to see the first bus leave. I flourished my handsome permit from the sardonic Colonel and sure enough I had a window seat. As we started north in the bright sun I felt on top of the world. Really cocky. A salt tang came from the Baltic but I didn't get a glimpse of it. A fair land, I thought, and I am going home. We broke down twice, and we stopped at every village and crossroads. I didn't care. I was once more on public transportation, I had seen telephones working and even seen a newspaper in Hamburg, though I couldn't buy one.

Soon it clouded up and began to drizzle. We went through Eutin and Malente, towns we had traveled through in the boxcar from Plön to Lütjenburg. We went east of Plön and the Plöner See and far south of Lütjenburg and on north to our destination, Preetz, about thirty-eight miles from Lübeck. Preetz was a county seat, lying southwest of Giekau, some fifteen miles away. We landed there around five o'clock in a drenching rain. I knew it was too late to find transportation now, so I made for the police station. It was small and cozy and friendly. The two old policemen (there seemed to be no young men yet on the German police force) took me in, astonished of course, but after explaining my predicament I told them I had established a precedent in Hamburg and had been so well entertained that, of course, I had come directly to them on arriving.

They made me at home on a dilapidated sofa, spread out my jacket and scarf to dry by the stove, and tugged off my boots. One man mysteriously left and reappeared with a covered pot of hot potato soup with meat in it and some bread and a little dish of stewed apples! I was very much touched. It was my first hot meal in five days.

The other policeman produced two carrots and we munched contentedly together. I slept soundly on my sofa without a thief or a prostitute to disturb me, and next morning I found my old boots all cleaned and polished. After breakfast I thanked them with tears in my eyes. I lost a paper with their names on it and could never send them anything later. But that wasn't the end of their kindness. They found a butcher who was driving to a village near Giekau and arranged for him to take me, and they gave me an idea.

They mentioned that Preetz was the food rationing and distribution center for our area, run by the Germans under direction of the British. I spent all morning with them, trying to wangle larger rations for Jerry and Erika. I flourished my *Schutzschein,* my passport, all my papers. I was very eloquent. I told them that the American Military Government, the British Military Government, and the Swiss Confederation all expected them, indeed ordered them, to supplement my American children's food supply.

At last they came across grudgingly with half a liter of milk and some margarine. It was the Swiss *Schutzschein* that really did it. I got out just in time for my rendezvous with the butcher at two o'clock. It was still cloudy but not raining, and we clopped along over the green hills contentedly silent. I had no trouble crossing into our Black Zone. Sitting beside the butcher, I was not questioned. He drove me a few miles out of his way but couldn't be persuaded to take me as far as Giekau, so I had to walk, but I was rested and on the home stretch.

As the church steeple appeared over the last hill, I suddenly realized that no one had the slightest idea when I would be back. I would be a surprise—and all the more fun. But I also remembered that, in spite of all reason, they expected me to bring back fantastic riches, perhaps arriving in a truck with American soldiers carrying in cartons of food, candy, and shoes. And what glamour did a couple more ration cards have for children? I knew even Dora had secret hopes, though unspoken. Still, I had an ecstatic welcome from Erika and Jerry and all the Lilienthals and had to tell my adventures over and over. There had been one mishap in my absence. Erika had scalded her foot carrying our kettle of hot soup with only one side handle left, and she still has the scar. I felt as if I had been gone a month.

Life was moving in Giekau, too. The British were sorting out our P.O.W.s and dividing them into the sheep and the goats. The officers were the goats. Unlike what I learned later to be the American policy, the British were sterner with the higher officers than with Nazi party members. Those of the rank of major and up were sent to special screening stations under heavy guard. Many of our friends were the first to go, including my three "students" beyond Dransau. Onkel Egon and the Hauptmann from Vienna were sent away separately to join other Austrians going home. The day the Captain left was very sad. After a last boat ride, he and Lotte had tea with Herr Pastor, and then off he was marched toward Lütjenburg. By the end of August only a few soldiers remained.

Early in September there was great rejoicing. Dora's husband, Fritz, sent word from a P.O.W. hospital that he had been badly wounded in the leg and foot before he was captured but would turn up as soon as possible. A clearing house for soldiers and their families had been established at last. Some refugee families were already leaving, those who lived west of the Russian Zone and had a place to go. But those from the East had to stay on. The natives were naturally glad to see each *Flüchtlinge* depart, so they could take a deep breath and get back to something like normal. The Pastorat family never made us feel unwelcome, for which I was very grateful.

Our joint money was running out now. We each had less than two hundred marks left. Not that we could buy much, but food cost something, and we each paid the Harmses fifteen marks rent per month. A peddler did come by one day, and we all bought some orange plastic butter dishes and a plate—the first thing we had seen to buy for two years except the ubiquitous ashtray.

One morning Hermann and Lütti rushed in in frantic excitement. Fritz had come at last! He was dark and very straight and tall, and very handsome, though gaunt and limping badly. His face was narrow and strong with a firm humorous mouth and the brightest and the blackest eyes I've ever seen!

Fortunately before he came, Lotte had been able to give Dora and me separate rooms, both upstairs, when some of the other families left. But we still ate together in Dora's room, which was larger, and did most of our cooking there, too, for she had a flat top stove for heat, which we could use for cooking. It was lucky that we all got on so well. We soon began to feel that we had always known him; and Jerry and Erika called him Onkel Fritz from the start. (Lütti called me "Tante Mary" but Hermann preferred "Aunt Mary.")

I grew more and more restless as September drew to a close. It was getting cold and would get colder, and the children were still running barefoot. I knew I had to have more money. I didn't really expect to hear from my Red Cross cards yet. The German post office finally opened, and I wrote a spate of letters to the only addresses I had for all the Jentsch family. My sister-in-law in Berlin answered promptly. She had stuck out the entire Battle of Berlin and all the previous months of incredible bombing. But she had no news of my husband, parents-in-law, or Rudolf and Ilse.

Another foray into the outside was due now, this time to Bremen, the U.S. enclave which was farther southwest than Hamburg, about a hundred and seventy-five miles from Giekau. I left in October, same boots and clothes, but I had to wear the old trek coat as it was quite cold. With difficulty I arranged with another P.O.W. quartermaster to take me part way. He was escorting a corpse to Neumünster.

I started this journey with less of the purely adventurous spirit and more grim determination. This time I had to succeed. At the border I simply said I thought my brother was in the American army at Bremen, and I had to see him about getting back. We got safely across, corpse and all, and drove by way of Kiel. Then on to Neumünster where the corpse and the quartermaster left me to hitchhike my way southwest to Bremen. I knew that my chances were small, as the hundreds of British army trucks that thundered along the highways were not allowed to take on civilians, and there were practically no German trucks on the roads. I had to depend on farmers' carts.

I was lucky, however, as I found two ramshackle German army trucks on errands southwest, and I got two long rides. All in all, I was in seven vehicles and made two overnight stops, one with the family of the farmer in whose wagon I was riding, and the other in a small railroad station. I didn't see a single bus.

The last short lap was made in a baker's small truck. He put me down in what had once been a suburb of Bremen, but not far from the center. Almost the first thing I noticed in the rubble was a brand new barracks—with the Stars and Stripes flying! I was trembling with excitement. For the first time in three years (except for Jane in Waren and the five-minute encounter with the young man in Hamburg) I would see my fellow countrymen. It was quite a moment, and I stood stock-still to savor it. I turned my back on the barracks and walked slowly down the street so as not to see any American soldiers until I had time to get ready. I'd pick a nice one and then speak to him in perfect American!

Several came out and passed me, brisk, pleasant-looking young men, walking with that easy, limber swing that is so un-European. They were joking unconcernedly together, unaware who was behind them. When I decided the moment had come, I turned and waited for another one to catch up with me.

"Can you tell me where to find your Commandant?"

"Commandant?" (My mistake.) "Your headquarters, your Commanding Officer. You see I'm an American, and I'd like to find out how to get back to the States." (My second mistake.)

"Headquarters is straight ahead for about a mile. Anyone will tell you where *Platz* is," he said and walked off quickly.

I considered my over-sized German boots and the kerchief bound tightly round my head, German-fashion. My face was rough and brown, long innocent of cold cream and lipstick. I looked like thousands of German refugee women and was obviously from the country. No pin-up girl for any G.I. And probably many Bremen women had learned a few phrases of English by now.

I found headquarters and that afternoon obtained a permit to get a pass to see someone in authority, but it was closing time and I'd have to wait until morning. Now the old problem of where to sleep. Not the German police station. It didn't seem dignified or fitting that I, an American among Americans, should ally myself with the Germans here. I asked a fat American major where I might stay overnight, briefly explaining my situation. He was surprised and scratched his head in a friendly fashion. He was darned if he knew and turned to a young soldier with him. There was a refugee barracks not far. He knew of nothing else. And that's where I stayed. It was just as crowded as the Hamburg place but not quite so dreary. They gave me bread and soup, and I slept on a bench.

I got into headquarters before the noon pause. Eventually I was sent to the third floor and once more told my threadbare tale. The fat colonel listened politely enough, though obviously very bored. But he questioned me sharply and gave me the familiar answer. No consulate opened yet, and so no one could screen me. I'd have to wait. No, he couldn't send a letter. It was against all regulations. "But I'm getting nowhere. You must help me, and..."

He rose in dismissal. I could see it was useless to argue with him. There was nothing for it but to leave. I sat on the grass in the *Platz* and ate some lunch from my rucksack.

This time I had brought double rations.

Perhaps my eye was jaundiced in my disappointment, but I was disillusioned. I hated to admit it, but in contrast to the British in Hamburg, lean, hard and fit, the older American men, especially the officers, all looked fat and soft and overfed. Only those under twenty-five looked slim and fit. I was quite surprised that my general impression was of a sallow lot of men, very different from my memory of twenty years back. Much later I was told that most of these troops had been sent over after the war, recruits fresh from training camps.

Again, what next? I would not go back to Giekau this time until something happened. My permit to headquarters was used up. I would walk around and keep my eyes open and sleep again if necessary at the German refugee camp. I stood up and adjusted my rucksack.

Then I saw an officer, tall and broad, but not fat! He had a determined chin, an intelligent open face, and alert, kind eyes. Everything about him looked kind. He had stopped a German boy on the street near me, whose face lighted up and who evidently knew him. As soon as they stopped talking, I walked boldly up to him.

"Have you time for me to speak to you for a few minutes?"

"Yes, of course. Why don't you come back to my office. It's just across the way."

It was as simple as that. We went upstairs to a large, pleasant room, and he introduced himself as Captain Charles Huston from Chicago. We talked for about three-quarters of an hour. I had made no mistake. I had picked out the kindest, most capable, and genuinely helpful man in all Bremen or anywhere else for that matter. He was brisk, business-like, and unsentimental. And his first impulse was action.

He talked so fast with such a pronounced Middle Western accent that I had great difficulty following him sometimes. Also, he joked in military jargon and a new and unfamiliar slang, which made me feel quite dumb. But nothing mattered. His decisions were always swift, and the red tape with which he was surrounded meant little to him. Above all, his approach to everything was fresh and unencumbered. It was against all regulations to send letters for civilians, American or otherwise, but give him a letter, two letters, and he'd send them off at once.

"Here. Sit down at my desk and write 'em now. Here's a pen and paper." No sooner said than done. I wrote to both Jake Beam and Tommy Thompson, asking them for advice and giving them Mother's last address. When I had finished, he sent for his young German secretary, Miss Duckwitz, a former student of Oriental languages. It was evident that she adored him, as did everyone who worked with him except the army red tapers. She came from an old Bremen family and a long line of distinguished citizens.

After scrawling notes to go with my letters, and sealing and stamping them then and there, Captain Huston suddenly barked to me, "Have you had any lunch?" When he heard my ration cards were not valid here, he called Magdalena Duckwitz. "Make out a card for that little restaurant up the street for Mrs. Jentsch. You won't find much, but it's something. Where are you staying?" I told him. "Well, go off to lunch now before it closes, and come back here and we'll see what we can do." Miss Duckwitz took us to wash up, telling me how wonderful he was, and then I sailed off to the restaurant, raised to dizzy heights. It was an indifferent lunch but at the time seemed to be the best I'd ever tasted.

"Now," he said, when I got back, "the letters have gone, and I've thought what you're to do. We'll get you and Erika and Jerry into the D.P. Camp here. I've read all your papers, and you're eligible." He asked me some pertinent questions and made a few notes. Business was over and he showed me photographs of his wife, Geneva, two daughters, Alice and Charlotte, and a boy, David. "Pretty nice looking lot. They write me all the time and send stuff for some of my Germans, gather clothes from all around—regular campaign. I'll see that you get something." He looked me over critically. "You certainly look as if you need some decent things."

He was quite amazed that we had come through alive. I left with another precious paper. "There isn't a free room in Bremen, but find your way to this address and give this note to the housekeeper. She'll put you up. No food there, though. Eat what you have in your rucksack for supper and come back here tomorrow morning. *Auf Wiedersehen*—and don't lose your way!"

Hooray for Americans, with a special hurray for Middle Westerners. My faith in my country soared as high as it had sunk low before lunch. After tramping quite a distance, I finally found the small, private house where I was to sleep. The comfortable German housekeeper received me in some consternation. It was reserved, she said, for American military passing through Bremen to and from Frankfurt and the American Zone proper in the south. But I was welcomed and put into a small, nicely furnished room, which, to me, seemed luxurious in the extreme. The house had the first central heating I'd seen since Berlin, and there was a real bathroom near my room. The housekeeper brought me some tea and a roll with a pat of margarine. I savored it while I exulted in my good fortune. Then I took a long, luxurious bath and washed my underthings. Just as I was coming out of the bathroom with my heavy coat over my nightgown, a soldier came out of his door.

"Hello," I said, and he muttered an astonished hello in return.

"American?"

"Yes," I replied, and he invited me into his room. It never occurred to me to hesitate, and we talked far into the night. From time to time he reached over and opened another box of K rations, which we munched absentmindedly as we talked and smoked. He was fascinated by my story and had to hear it over and over with all its details. He told me about his work in Frankfurt and his war experiences in the Battle of the Bulge. It had been so long since he'd talked to an American woman and since I had talked to any American, we wound up exchanging the intimate stories of our lives. I left at last, talked out and very sleepy with his parting gift of several packages of cigarettes.

Next morning after a breakfast of real coffee, rolls, and an egg, I was back in Captain Huston's office where he gave me my permit to enter the D.P. Camp. We decided that I should get myself and the children there on November 1. He told me he was in charge of German civilian prisons in the enclave and was kept busy going from one to the other. Being very practical and very impatient, he was frustrated much of the time by the red tape. Not an Army man by nature or profession, he was looking forward to returning to the U.S. and the insurance business.

He gave me another ticket to the restaurant and told me he'd found me a ride to Neumünster. As he left, he thrust some chocolate bars, K rations, peanuts, chewing gum, a few apples, and a pair of German cotton stockings into my hands, which was all he had at the moment. Miss Duckwitz added a little package of powdered coffee. I was jubilant at having something tangible to take back to the children.

* * * * * *

We were to enter the D.P. Camp on November 1, so we had a little more than two weeks left in Giekau. Captain Huston had tried to lend me money, but after he told me that the camp would be free, I had refused it. I had a hundred marks left and since the children and I would be taking the few possessions we had left, I found a man who would take us in his car—for one hundred marks.

The day before we left was Halloween—and Jerry's seventh birthday. Dora made a splendid celebration; she even made marzipan. But though our last night together was gay and warm, it was also sad. I was going home to live once more the life of an American. Erika and Jerry would be brought up as citizens of the U.S.A.

But for Dora and Fritz the future looked hopeless. Fritz had a double handicap. His leg and foot were partially crippled, and his profession had vanished. He had been trained to manage his big estate in East Prussia, now gone along with many others. The only other job he'd ever held had been as an Army officer.

There were many men like Fritz who found themselves in West Germany after the war, the land where they had their estates now a part of Poland. Germany was shrunk to one third her former size, and most of the West was industrial. Though Fritz and Dora were ready to work, there was nothing for them to do. There might have been possibilities beyond the confines of Giekau, but no one was allowed to leave his present "home" without the guarantee of another room and a job. With returning soldiers flooding the job market and joining the exiles from the East in the search for housing, there was little hope for a change.

Early in the morning of November 1, a bleak, cold day with snow to come, we said our farewells. All our friends came to see us off, the Harmses, the Jägers, everyone. It was a cheerful and a tearful sendoff. We sang our old theme song, "*Ich wäre so gerne geblieben, Aber der Wagen der rollt*," and never had it seemed so poignant. A final wave and we were off, around the curve, past Neuhaus, then the wood and the end of the lake and onto the high road.

Chapter Seven

BREMEN
November 1945 to June 1946
The Road Home

ALTHOUGH THE WAR HAD ENDED, the chaos in Germany continued. The Nuremberg Trials were underway, and the Allies were consolidating their spheres of influence within defeated Germany. As the Americans and Russians began a confrontation that later turned into the Cold War, the plight of German civilians became an afterthought.

Leaving Giekau, we drove along steadily with our taciturn companion. He was not a good driver, and as it began to snow heavily he drove more recklessly. The car broke down once on the great *Autobahn,* and I was afraid we wouldn't make it. And our clothes! What would they think of us in the camp? But then I thought of good food and plenty of it, no fires to tend, and best of all, Captain Huston, our friend.

It stopped snowing as we came into Bremen just before dusk. Neither the driver nor I knew the city, and we had some difficulty finding Tirpitz D.P. Camp. We were told to follow a long busy street with tram rails, which we did. The driver grumbled that he would be late for his appointment, as we crossed the Weser River and drove for some miles out of town.

Our first sight of Tirpitz was so grim that we all three wanted to turn around and drive straight back to Giekau. A piece of land fenced off with high wire held acres of low, wooden barracks. A bright light at the gate and the dim bulb over the doorway of each building looked cheerless and uninviting. The driver dumped our motley baggage in front of the office. I paid him my last hundred marks, and he was off.

We went in and found an Englishman who greeted us and looked at our credentials, then turned us over to a Polish woman. We dragged our stuff across the frozen ground to a barracks and down a long, dimly lit corridor into a great dormitory with two tiers of bunks. The woman pulled together three cots and a double-decker bed provided with two army blankets apiece, told us they were ours, and left. She said we were too late for supper, but we could come back to the office and get something.

The room smelled foul and was as dirty as it smelled. It was full of Polish men, women, and children in all stages of undress, and the air was blue with cigarette smoke. They looked at us curiously for a moment, then turned back to their noisy chatter.

I asked in English where the washroom was and found it was at the far end of the corridor. Tirpitz had been built for a German naval training center, I learned later, but had been a D.P. Camp under UNRRA (United Nations Relief and Rehabilitation Association) since the end of the war. The washroom was a large place with bowls at one end and lines of open toilets. Not one had been closed off for women, though at least the showers were enclosed.

We got bread and Spam at the office, and to the wonderment of Erika and Jerry, an orange apiece. Reluctantly we found our way back to our dormitory, now fuller than ever. Some of the people were friendly enough, but I was aghast at the noise and dirt. We distributed our baggage under our bunks, got out our night things, and tried to sleep. I put my briefcase under my pillow. In spite of the talking, laughing, singing, and lovemaking, we slept soundly all night.

Next morning we woke at our usual hour but found everyone else sound asleep. We had to use our own towels in the washroom. From then on I never let Erika go alone to the toilet. We stood in front of each other. Before we got our breakfast, we were summoned to the office, were given ration cards with our names and camp numbers on them, and sent to the mess hall.

Behind a long counter, men were handing out food. We received five long loaves of dark bread, an eighth of a pound of butter, a paper twist of sugar and two large cans of Spam. This was our daily ration for breakfast and supper combined. Then we were each given a tin cup filled with real coffee! I asked about milk for the children and was told, "Bring your own can. There are plenty of empty cans out on the dump heap just beyond the last barrack."

We were supposed to eat our food in the dormitory, where there were several long tables. We crowded in with our roommates that first breakfast, and I tried to get on friendly terms with them. Only one spoke any English, and, not surprisingly given their feelings about Germans, they were suspicious of us when the children spoke German to them and refused to answer. We gorged ourselves and then, after breakfast, went out to find tin cans on the dump heap, a glittering mountain of silver and gold. We selected five quart-sized tins (the smallest there): one for milk, one each for soup or stew, and one for coffee. The next day I found a Latvian who bored holes in them and made wire handles. We had no place to store our surplus food and had to put it in a suitcase. Erika and Jerry were very much subdued, and I was bitterly disappointed in the camp.

We spent the morning being questioned by an English-speaking Pole and having our photographs and thumb prints taken. We were also given some shots (I never knew what for) and sprayed all over with D.D.T. At dinnertime, we took our quart cans to the canteen, where everyone else was swinging cans that held a half-gallon. Our cards were checked off with an X for each item as our cans were filled with a rich meat stew, then boiled potatoes and, on top of that, cabbage. Though it was excellent and we gorged ourselves, we couldn't eat more than one third of it. Nor could we save it, though it went against the grain not to. We had to throw most of it into the biggest garbage cans in the longest row I have ever seen, cans filled with whole loaves of bread and half-full tins of Spam. It was the same every day, a criminal waste that we found horrifying.

For supper there was real coffee again and hot soup and cheese and an apple apiece. The food was so wonderful and abundant that while we were greedily filling ourselves, we forgot our loneliness and simply exulted in our good fortune. We soon learned that our stomachs had shrunk and that we could eat less than we thought.

When we came back from the washroom that night along the dimly lit corridor, I found to my horror that the threshold was occupied by a couple making love. Indeed, the whole room was filled with disorderly couples, many of them drunk. I told the children stories frantically until they were asleep.

Next morning on my way to the office to protest, a nice looking woman came hurrying towards me. "Mrs. Jentsch?" She told me she was an Australian UNRRA worker and had just come back last night from a work trip. She had heard I was here and realized the situation without my telling her. "Yes, yes, I know, and I've found a cubby-hole for you three alone."

We ran back and got our belongings, and she took us to a small office in another dormitory. "I'll have three cots put in here for you, and there's just room for a little table and chair." I have never been so relieved nor so grateful. It was heaven. There was also a little black stove with coal. There were radiators in the barracks, but evidently the fuel for the central building had given out long ago and the whole place was heated with iron stoves.

Our friend explained that this camp had been full of many nationalities, forced labor mostly, who had all been repatriated months ago. Now there was only a small contingent of displaced Latvians, Lithuanians, and Estonians who could not go back home. The other ninety percent were Poles who would not go back and wanted to go to the United States. Most of these had been in forced labor camps for years and then in D.P. camps since the end of the war. They were completely demoralized. They were given no work to do, no classes to attend, and by now were surfeited with good food, rest, and cigarettes, so they kept occupied by getting into mischief.

I said that I understood and that I was very grateful to be here, that the food and shelter were wonderful and everything was fine now that we had our own room. Next day she came again and brought the children a can of orange juice and some oranges. Then she was whisked away to some other trouble spot, and we never saw her again. After about a week of trying to eat all our five loaves of bread, I told the man at the canteen who gave out our morning bread, butter, and milk rations, that we didn't need five loaves and that two would be ample.

"You don't want your good bread? Okay then, don't take any butter!" I thought he was joking but he meant it, so we continued to take five loaves every day for the sake of the butter. I couldn't send them to Dora or give them to anyone else, so we, too, threw good food into the garbage cans. I have never felt more alone. After our bustling crowded life in Giekau and our happy companionship with the Lilienthals and other friends, life was dreary and boring in the extreme for all three of us. It was cold and muddy in the bleak windswept areas outside, and our room was so tiny we couldn't stay there all the time. We walked briskly round and round as a duty, but it was no fun. Erika and Jerry played with the Baltic children, but they weren't the right ages. Occasionally they played with a Polish child, but the Poles had evidently been warned not to play with German-speaking children.

I organized a class for Jerry, Erika, and two Latvian children and procured some blank books at the office. It didn't last long, and Erika and Jerry used the blank books for drawing pictures and writing a little English. I read Our Book (*The Jungle Book*) to them at least fifty times. Leisure and good food were fine, but one could not survive on them alone. The worst of all was that there was no one to answer our questions. How long would we have to stay? Had the American Consulate opened in Bremen? What was the news in the world, and why didn't I receive answers to my letters and postcards? I couldn't even find out exactly how far out we were from Bremen. But I did know that we couldn't leave the grounds without a permit from some authorized person on the outside.

After about ten days I was called to the office. There was a letter for me, a very formal little note from an unknown English officer enclosing one hundred German marks. My old friend, Jacob Beam of the State Department (now Ambassador to Warsaw), had requested him to send the money to me as I was in the British Zone. My first outside communication! I was deeply touched and excited. At least one card or letter had got through.

A few days later, I was told that Captain Huston had requested that the three of us be given a permit to come into Bremen. We made the greatest preparations for our day out. I was amazed to discover that there was actually a tram near the gate that took us straight into town. We were greeted heartily by Chuck and Magdalena Duckwitz. Chuck handed me a message to call Jim Wharton, who was in Berlin on a mission from the State Department. We had known Jim, a freelance newspaperman, during the Paris years, and my friend Esther Forbes, having learned where I was, had given him Captain Huston's address. Magdalena put the call through and in a moment I heard Jim's warm, familiar voice. Now my old friends and family knew where we were and were doing everything they could to help.

December was a cold month with chill winds blowing from the North Sea, but we were warm and fairly cozy in our little room, drawing, telling stories, and learning to read English via *The Jungle Book*. This is when I invented the "Janey" stories, a serial of which there must have been some hundred installments. It was not very original, an incongruous mixture of my grandmother's animal tales and my favorite childhood books. But Erika and Jerry both loved Janey. There was also a more childish saga begun in Geneva about Zip and Goat, which was still acceptable to Jerry, and stories of my own happy childhood in Louisville. We discovered by pure chance that movies were presented twice a week in the big recreation room. They were all American movies and were, without exception, Hollywood's most lurid crime films. Erika and Jerry liked the novelty at first, for they had not seen more than three shows in their lives and those had been fairy and puppet shows given for children in Berlin.

One day a Latvian acquaintance passed on a rumor that three Poles had got through the fence the night before and murdered a German farm family, then returned to the camp. Some of the Poles, who had been cruelly and brutally treated by the Germans, talked with glee about what they considered a daring feat. We believed the story and were fearful that with their plentiful supply of liquor and the shocking negligence of the camp authorities, anything could happen. I never let the children wander far from me, kept my briefcase slung around my neck, and barricaded our door at night with the table, as we had no lock.

Christmas was upon us but we were not looking forward to it until we received an invitation from Captain Huston to a Christmas party at the Bohles', another family he had befriended. Ruth Bohle was an American from Chicago, whose German husband had been drafted into the German Army. In a flight similar to mine, they had managed to get to Bremen after the war ended. The Hustons knew Ruth's family, and Chuck had found Ruth a job with the Army of Occupation, while trying to help them get to the United States. He was also trying to get Ruth's husband,

Hans, an artificial leg to replace the one he had lost in the war. Christmas dinner, furnished by Captain Huston, was gay and festive, and we liked the Bohles, whose several children included a girl Erika's age and a boy the same age as Jerry. There were presents for everyone sent by Mrs. Huston from Flossmoor, Illinois—stockings, socks, hair ribbons, soap, and even some little toys.

There was another, belated Christmas present for Mary. Jim Wharton and Jake Beam had managed to locate Gerhart. He had been captured and was in the American Zone, but he was still alive and was able to telephone Mary from Bavaria. Although only those two know exactly what was said in that call, a few months later he wrote to his friend, John Rothschild, recounting his experiences after he had disappeared. It is, stripped of emotion, the story he must have told his wife:

"In January 1945, the company in which I served as courier and liaison man had to defend an island in the Oder in Upper Silesia; we were cut off by the Russians and shelled day and night. We lay in the snow, without winter equipment: for about ten days I survived by incessantly turning my hands and feet at a rhythm that kept the heart going. When the Russian infantry started its concentric attack, I suddenly realized I was the only German still alive on the island. So I covered myself with snow as best I could, leaving only my eyes free. They did not notice me and passed on. When they were gone, I rolled myself close to the ruins of a house which they had set on fire, in order to get warm and be able to stand. I then realized I had high fever and pneumonia.

During the nights that followed, I made my way westward in an effort to reach our lines again. I have only the haziest recollection of those nights because my fever wrought havoc on the realities around and within me. When my mind came clear again, I was on our side at a dressing station in Matrish-Ostran [Moravska Ostrava, Czechoslovakia]. I was given a fever thermometer, a handful of quinine to handle the fever, and a ticket to Dresden where I was to report at a hospital. I arrived in Dresden on the night the British or U.S. air force destroyed the central railway station and the inner city. I am one of the very few survivors among the 10 to 15,000 people who perished when the high vaulted roof of the station came crashing down. Next morning, I failed to get admitted to a hospital. I got a few injections, more quinine, and a ticket to Munich. I arrived unconscious but still alive, as I discovered a week after my arrival there.

In the first week of May, I was well again, except for a touch of TB. I then started south in order to join some outfit in the Alps. I had reached Rottach-Egern on the Tegernsee when the capitulation occurred. A few days later, I was taken prisoner by the U.S. 54th Armored Infantry Battalion. It so happened that the Commanding Officer of that battalion just then needed an interpreter and that interpreter I became. I was well treated and well fed and billeted in a private room, just like the officers for whom I worked. I consider that I owe my restored health to this, for good lodging and good food were responsible for my getting over my TB.

In the middle of July, 1945, the 54th were recalled to the USA. Major Haskell, the commander, wrote me a splendid testimonial for my services as interpreter, on the strength of which I got my discharge into civilian life.

I started out possessing exactly one old uniform, two sets of underwear, one pair of shoes, three handkerchiefs, one blanket, and some toilet articles. I had had news in June from eyewitnesses that the house where I had lived in Beeskow, the house where I had stored the rest of my belongings, the library office, and the church with the library had all been burned when the Russians took the town. My insurances and my bank account are likewise gone."

Readers will certainly have noticed the striking absence of Gerhart from Mary's narrative. From the text, it would appear that she saw nothing of him for the duration of the war, when in fact the family shared an apartment in Berlin as late as 1943, at least during the winter months. After Mary and the children left Berlin, he regularly wrote to them until the final months of the war and resumed contact with the phone call mentioned above. Yet no plans for a reunion are recorded.

Gerhart, then and later, urged Mary "to separate your fate and the children's from mine and to return to the U.S. There's no point having the children grow up here." It must have been a hard decision. In at least one letter to a friend in *the United States, Mary mentions the possibility of staying in Germany, of being near Gerhart. But she has chosen badly once for her children, following her husband into a war. This time she chooses a future apart.*

In the last days of the war, Gerhart had taken refuge on a farm owned by the parents of Hilde Dinkgraeve, his secretary in Beeskow, whom he would later marry, after divorcing Mary in 1946. We can only speculate whether, like the German soldiers in the Geikau who fell into quick and intense romances, Gerhart had found a new love with Hilde, or whether the end of the war and eventual departure of his family made him turn to her.

The first week in February we learned that Camp Tirpitz was to be abandoned. We were to be sent to another D.P. camp farther south in the American Zone. No one could find out where these other camps were or which of them we were to be sent to and I determined not to go, but I was unable to reach Chuck, who was out of town.

We were to be out of Camp Tirpitz on February 10, and I was beginning to despair when, at the very last minute, Chuck returned and sent a message saying that he'd send a truck to pick us up and move our belongings into Bremen. He had found a little flat for us and a job for me. When I informed our Commandant that I wouldn't be going with the others, he didn't seem to care, but he said we must be out by eight p.m. when the Military were taking over.

There was feverish activity all the day before, with everyone dragging out cots, blankets, chairs, and even stoves complete with stovepipes. Early on the tenth (Erika's eleventh birthday and a cold and cloudy one) a dozen huge trucks appeared, the first one pulling out immediately with the canteen, food, and all the equipment. Then the Poles and Baltic families piled their loot in, amidst wild confusion and noise, and clambered atop it. By the middle of the afternoon the camp was empty. At four o'clock we went over to the office; only one woman remained.

"Haven't you gone yet?" she asked.

"No, but our truck will come soon," I told her.

"Well, you have to be out by eight, when the Military come."

When I said we had no dinner, she pointed out that the kitchen had left right after breakfast. "I am leaving at five. I'm the last one." She gave me two oranges (there had been only coffee and milk given out at breakfast) and said goodbye. Just before five I went back and asked if she could call Captain Huston, but she couldn't get through to Bremen.

She left, and we were alone in the camp. We hurried back to our room, feeling abandoned and frightened as dusk closed in over the acres of bare ground and empty, dark barracks. While there was still some light, I decided to follow the others' example. After searching several barracks, I found a nice little stove. Captain Huston's message had warned me that there was as yet no stove in our flat, so the three of us dragged it over to our quarters. Our mattresses were already rolled up and ready to be taken out with the cots when the truck came. But no truck appeared.

It was now night, and I found to my horror that the electricity was turned off. There was not one light in the whole camp. Our room was cold, as I had neglected to lay in a supply of coal the day before. We ate our bread and margarine and walked up and down outside our door to keep warm. At eight we went back to the gate. Still no sign of the Military, and I didn't tell the children that we were locked in. I had tried the gate. The wind was too cold to stay there long, so we went back to our room once more.

It was scary to walk across that vast, open parade ground with the long barracks empty all around us. About nine-thirty we walked to the gate once more and discovered two G.I.s setting up a sentry box. I called out to them as we approached (my imagination was by now so lively that I thought they might point their guns at us). They were startled to hear an American voice and sympathetic when I explained our plight. When I told them that we would probably have to stay all night and that I was frightened, they promised to patrol the camp during the night. One of them gave me a couple of cigarettes, and we went back much comforted and resolved to go to bed.

We lay down on the mattresses with our coats on and wrapped our blankets around us. I told stories until Erika and Jerry got to sleep. We were far from the gate, too far for the soldiers to hear us. I thought of the story about the murderers, and then of how some Germans, knowing the camp had been abandoned, might try to get in to loot what was left. I couldn't see my watch, but twice during the night I heard the reassuring tramp of a soldier's boots. Finally I dozed off.

We were awakened by a loud crash and a bright blaze of light shining in our eyes. I was paralyzed and must have screamed at the sight of a dark figure climbing over the barricade I'd erected. But it wasn't a murderer; it was Chuck come to tell us that the river Weser, which lay between the camp and Bremen, had flooded and washed out the bridge, making it impossible for the truck to get through. Chuck hadn't learned this until very late, and it had taken him hours in a jeep to get through. He couldn't take us and our baggage back with him because of the flood, but he left us food and a flashlight and the promise that early the next morning the bridge would be repaired and we would be taken to Bremen. The guards, he said, would be on frequent patrol for the rest of the night. We ate the cheese, *Wurst*, and oranges he had brought for Erika's special birthday dinner and then, completely reassured, we slept.

Next morning, carrying our household goods and the pilfered stove, we took possession of our new quarters, kitchen privileges plus two rooms and a bath on the top floor of a private house in Hagenauer Strasse. We were just three doors from the Bohles'. Gas and electricity could only be turned on for short periods. Gas, especially, was very scarce. We shared the stove with two other refugee families and had it for an hour in the morning, two hours at noon, and one at night. Because of my job, I got up early and started our little stove for heat, then went to the kitchen to warm milk for the children to drink with their bread and margarine or cheese. Then I left them to their own devices for the day and got the tram downtown to my office.

Gerhart had managed to send Erika a birthday letter, which finally reached her:
  "I wish that you will never again in the future need to experience such a wild year as the last has been. Flight and life-threatening danger: hopefully you will be spared these in the future. This is the last birthday that you will have in Germany.... I wish that things will go better for you in America and will please you well and that you will be a good and loyal American girl.... I am sure that you will have a beautiful and hap-

py birthday celebration in the camp....I am very sorry that I can't send anything—except for my thoughts which are full of love for you."

Some schools had reopened in Bremen, but there was such a dearth of buildings, teachers, textbooks, and materials that the children only went for two hours a day, and only the teacher had a textbook. After school Erika and Jerry took our Tirpitz pails to a soup kitchen several blocks away and got their main meal, soup or stew, on their ration cards. I supposed they took it straight home and ate it, as it was a cold February, but I found out later that they usually sat on the curbstone and ate it cold.

Erika then played with Irmgard Bohle in a warm room, but Jerry and Dieter Bohle found a neighborhood gang of little boys who owned two express wagons among them. They went tearing all over our section of town, pulling and pushing the wagons, jumping on and off trams, and miraculously dodging the innumerable military jeeps driven at terrific speed. The most dangerous fun they had was playing in ruined buildings with *Verboten* signs on them. They climbed up shaky walls and pipes, which at any moment could have toppled over and killed them, also discovering charred bodies. A natural for little boys and I am glad I didn't know about it.

Jerry remembers Bremen as heaven, when he was free as a bird from morning until night to roam where and with whom he pleased. Erika tried to look after him but gave up. She usually managed to corral him at nightfall and get him home. I got home a bare half hour or twenty minutes before the gas went off and often couldn't finish the porridge I started for their supper. I was all right. As an employee of the Army of Occupation, I had a free lunch on the American government, but the children were on German rations and were not getting one third of the food they had at camp.

Chuck made many clandestine visits to us and to the Bohles, appearing after dark like Santa Claus, dragging up two flights of stairs a heavy sack of briquettes for our stove, cans of powdered milk, sugar, and any other exotic delicacy he could lay his hands on. This was illicit traffic in Army food, and he could have had a severe penalty for it, but without him Jerry and Erika and the Bohle children would have had a bad time. He always appeared at the right moment to cheer us up with his jokes and gaiety, as well as the food.

At my job I was put to work translating long questionnaires—about fifty-nine questions, many of them requiring several paragraphs of answers—which had previously been filled out by Germans. This was the preliminary de-Nazification process. There were about six of us in my office: Germans who had already been de-Nazified and several Jewish refugees from concentration camps. It was depressing work, but I was glad to have the job.

There were two cafeterias a block or so away for government workers, one for the non-Germans (mostly Poles and Czechs), who received more abundant food, and the other for Germans. Ruth Bohle and I ate with the Germans, as our status was not yet defined. After the primitive facilities of the camp, it seemed like dining at the Ritz. We also got breakfast there at 8:15, and that was the best of all. Two cups of real coffee, cold cereal, even orange juice, and sometimes bacon. Ruth and I felt badly because we couldn't take home our rolls and margarine to the children, but we were not allowed to take out any of our uneaten food.

Soon after our installation in Bremen, Chuck wangled

a memorable shopping expedition. During our time at the camp, we had not been given new clothes and shoes. Besides our boots and wooden clogs, I had a disreputable pair of brown oxfords, resoled by amateurs many times and patched on the uppers. But our visit with Chuck to an UNRRA warehouse was more sumptuous and exciting than Macy's. There were no dresses left, but Erika and I each got a very good English mackintosh and cotton stockings. I also got what was called a "lumber jacket," a short, heavy, cotton twill jacket lined with blue wool with a hood.

Apparently all our UNRRA food was from America, while all the clothes were contributed by England. Now we all had spring coats. Best of all, we got shoes, not very chic, but then everybody was wearing the same sort. The soles were of wood, but the uppers were leather. I still had no decent dress to wear to work, but soon a skirt and two blouses, and two nice cotton dresses for Erika came through from Mrs. Huston. She must have been indefatigable in collecting clothes, as the Bohles, all of Chuck's office staff, and many of his German friends wore clothes from Flossmoor, Illinois.

Sometime in April, an American consulate opened in Bremen, but it was not until the very end of May that Ruth Bohle and I were screened—and not until June that we knew definitely we could leave Germany. In the meantime I had been cheered by warm letters and messages from Mother, my sister Elizabeth, my old friend Esther Forbes, and one from another old friend, Mary Allen, offering to sponsor us and take us into her home in Worcester. Massachusetts. My mother was ill (I didn't know how ill at the time; she died soon after we arrived in America.) and it was a godsend to be sponsored and have a place to go.

When we received our precious new refugee passports,

I began to pack in a daze. I had made some good friends among my German fellow-workers in the office, and they had a party for the children and me and gave us little souvenirs of Bremen. Magdalena invited us to her house one evening, and Chuck bid us farewell the last night. We went to a sort of embarkation camp in Bremen for two days, where we were given physical exams, various shots, and our sailing papers. It was not a particularly pleasant trip—we were in a bunk room with about six sets of three-tiered bunks—but what were ten days of discomfort to six years?

Mary and Gerhart met at least once before parting. Their son writes: "I saw my father in 1946 in Bremen just before my mother, sister, and I left for America. All I can remember is that he hugged my mother and patted her on the back, which for some reason I never forgot. For a long time I expected him to return."

Sometime during the day of June 26, we steamed past the faraway coast of Martha's Vineyard, then along Long Island, and before dawn of the next day we entered New York Harbor. That day Jerry and Erika stood on U.S. soil for the first time. After eighteen years, I was home.

Epilogue

by Steve Mumford

ALTHOUGH MY GRANDMOTHER would now have to start her life over again, at least she had arrived safely in America with her two children. She was able to see her mother before she died and reunite with her siblings. However, she went to live with her old friend Mary Allen, who had offered to sponsor her return to the U.S.

My grandmother spent the rest of her life—twenty-six years—living at the large Allen home in Worcester, Massachusetts. My mother, Erika, and Uncle Jerry grew up and went to school there. My grandmother never remarried.

Gran would come to Boston, where we lived in a converted 19th-century firehouse near Beacon Hill. In the mornings my brother and I would dash from our room to hers, still in our pajamas, and jump on the bed.

"Morning, Gran, good morning! Tell us a story!"

Smiling, she'd smooth out the bedspread and take out a Kent. I loved watching her smoke. I liked the way she smelled, and that morning cigarette had a wonderfully comforting air to it. Her voice was strong and crisp, like her mind, but with a gravelly, sonorous edge perhaps from her smoking. Her strong mouth always seemed to have a slight smile playing over it.

"What shall I tell you about?" she mused. "Would you like a story from when your Gran was a little girl in Kentucky? Or maybe you'd like to hear about little Hans. Hans was one of your mother's schoolmates when we were in Germany during the war. He was a very nice little boy but he never washed his ears. Ever! Then one day he came over to visit Erika, and I noticed a small twig with a tiny leaf was growing from his ear..."

As hard as the war experience had been, Gran once wrote: "It was the most interesting period of my life, if not the pleasantest. The children and I learned the inner peace of country life; that there is always hope; that you don't know what you can stand or what you can do until you have to. And what you can do without. We were among the lucky ones. We came through whole."

What Happened to Them All

Back in the U.S. after the war, Gran tried to track down what had happened to the people with whom she had spent those harrowing years. She got in touch with her sister-in-law, Lonny, by writing to their old address in Berlin. Lonny and Walter were still in the same apartment house, although every other one in the block had gone down.

She learned that Gerhardt's parents, with whom she had sought refuge in Silesia, were dead. "After the Russians took Silesia," Mary writes, "it was turned over to the Poles, but Vater and Mutter Jentsch stayed on. Vater was too ill to make a long, hard journey into an uncertain future. Then late in 1945 or early in 1946, the Poles did to the Germans what the Germans had done to them: they turned out those who were too old or too ill to work. It was winter when Vater and Mutter left, walking over the mountains, westward. Vater was feeble, and Mutter had bad arthritis in her legs.

"Somewhere in the Rissengebirge, Vater died and was buried there by the roadside. Mutter toiled on, though without Vater the rest of the long, hard trip seemed pointless. She died some months later in Bavaria. Not only Vater was gone. Her whole world had vanished, and I suspect that she died not of the hardship but of a broken heart.

"The *Flüchtlinge* (refugees) from the East had a tougher time than even the Westerners who were bombed out. They lost everything and were not wanted in the West, where they had few relatives. Those from east of the Oder and the Neisse Rivers had the roughest going of all. Very few refugees got in on the economic boom in West Germany—only those with some very special talents and luck.

"The Lilienthal Trek from Caymen in East Prussia (*which Mary's traveling companion Dora Lilienthal had hoped, in vain, to meet up with in Waren*) arrived in the West sometime in the summer of 1945 after many vicissitudes. But we knew nothing until the fall, owing to the breakdown of all communication. Fritz's mother, the heart and soul of the expedition, had died of typhus somewhere in the East, and Dora's mother was very ill for months.

"Dora and Fritz Lilienthal were forced to stay in Giekau until the middle 1950's, when Fritz finally found a job in Bonn, though not adequate to his abilities. Life remained difficult for them, but the boys (*Ernst and Hermann, their brave companions on the trek*) put themselves through school, with Ernst (Lütti) working as a mining engineer and Hermann finishing the University of Bonn.

"I finally got in touch with Else Wegener (*Mary's good friend, who ran the general store in Barnimskunow. Their ways had parted in Mulkenthin, still east of the Oder, when Mary and Dora and their children had hitched a last-minute ride with some German soldiers heading west.*) while I was in Tirpitz Camp, and I learned her adventures from the time we had left the Barnimskunow Trek so precipitately.

"The Trek had left Mulkenthin and with great difficulty got across the Oder. Else's wagon and several others bat-

tened down in a village in Vor-Pommern to await the end
of the war. This was near the river, not very far as the crow
flies from Barnimskunow (which lay across the Oder and
some fifteen miles to the east). They figured on returning
to Barnimskunow when the fighting ended, thinking one
place was as good as another, the nearer the better, and never dreaming that at war's end Pommern (East Pommern)
would be handed over to the Poles.

"There they stayed until the Russians crossed the Oder.
Trying to escape, they managed to get to a point some miles
north, near the Baltic, before they were overtaken. Else's invalid brother was taken off and never seen again, as were
their horse and wagon. Else, her children Eva and Ernst,
and her sister Lise, were put to work in the fields under the
Russians. Their forced labor may have been a rough justice,
but it was hard that it had to be applied to Else and Lise,
who were not young and had been kind to the Russians.

"During those first months, Else made her daughter,
Eva, spend every night hiding under the bed, while Else lay
on top of it to protect her. Both women escaped rape, but
Else received several knife slashes from drunken soldiers.
Some months later both Lise and their 80-year-old aunt
died. Else herself was ill for months with typhus. When that
first drunken onslaught abated, the Wegeners got themselves moved to a small town further west, though still in
the Russian Zone. Else got a job as housekeeper and gardener for an old German lady, and Ernst worked as a farmhand. A year later Eva went to the British sector of Berlin
and lived with old friends of her mother's while she worked
as an apprentice seamstress in a dressmaking establishment,
making clothes for the wives of the Russian officers.

"Else's dream was to be reunited with Eva and Ernst,

and finally in 1958 all three moved to Münster in Westfalen, a beautiful, old city north of Cologne. Ernst married, continued to farm, and Eva, having passed her apprenticeship examination in Berlin, became a professional dressmaker.

"Frau Schwarz and her wild brood reached her parents' home in Pasewalk in Vor-Pommern and then got out again before the Russians came. She landed in the northwest corner of Schleswig on the North Sea. Herr Pastor Schwarz eventually returned, producing a seventh child—little Irene. (Gottfried, the sixth, was born in Barnimskunow about two months before we left).

"They stayed in Schleswig for some years then left for a parish in a suburb of Hamburg. Ernst-Wilhelm, the bad egg and his mother's darling, left home after working in the mines and married without his parents' approval; Christian entered the merchant marines; and Jürgen, Jerry's friend, did service in the navy. Puppe Pastor, now Ilse-Maria, gave up her agricultural career and started on a theatrical career, but she was deflected by a native of the West Indies. The last I heard, she intended to marry him and return with him to the islands. Little Crista, it was said, was rebelling for a freer life. There was always drama in the Schwarz family.

"Herr Hecker (*the* Inspecktor *who had to stay longer in Barnimskunow in order to turn the landowner's estate over to the* Wehrmacht) and his bicycle never caught up with the Trek. He was, I believe, captured by the Russians. Much later he found his family near Magdeburg in the central part of Germany in the Russian Zone. The old Tante and Oncle did not survive the Trek, dying somewhere along the way.

"The Jürgens, my Waren family, fared worst of all. When I got to America I wrote to Frau Hanni and after some time got a letter from her daughter. Their father and brother had been killed in the war, and Frau Hanni herself had been raped by several Russians in her kitchen under the eyes of her helpless old mother. The next day the old lady hanged herself. I have never heard from Frau Hanni herself and lost contact with the daughter, who married and moved away.

"We stopped to visit Charles Huston in Flossmoor, Illinois, on our way to Wyoming in 1949 and had the great pleasure of meeting his wife Geneva. In the spring of 1951, Chuck and Geneva drove East for their daughter's graduation at Mount Holyoke College. All three spent the weekend with us. It was a gay and happy reunion. Several years later Charles Huston died of a heart attack. I lost a real friend."

The Jentsch Family

In June 1946, as my grandmother and her children sailed for America, Gerhart was working as a manager and liaison in a Southern Bavarian quarry that produced railroad ballast and road gravel. He doubted whether he'd ever be able to return to academic life. As Germany returned to a more normal state after the war, though, he found work as one of the senior English-German translators for official documents at the foreign office of the *Bundesrepublik* in Bonn.

Gerhart and Mary were divorced in 1946, and the next year my grandfather married Hilde Dinkgraeve, the woman who had been his secretary in Beeskow. I have often wondered: was this a simple case of a man leaving his wife and children for a younger woman, albeit against the backdrop of world war? Or were both Mary and Gerhart simply exhausted and demoralized, needing above all to return home and be among their own people?

Gerhart was German to the core; his personal fortunes

seemed to mirror those of his native land. At eighteen, he left his studies to volunteer for service on the front lines in World War I. Subsequently, his family lost all their money in a bank collapse. As Germany's inflation grew worse, Gerhart had moved to the United States, studying at Harvard University and earning enough money on the side to send home. He was eventually offered an assistant professorship in the Harvard history department but turned it down (in part because he'd be expected to "assimilate into the Anglo-Saxon world"), just as he turned down subsequent offers.

His longtime friend and business partner John Rothschild was Jewish, so I don't believe Gerhart was anti-Semitic. Yet he and Mary arrived in Berlin a year after *Kristallnacht*, four years after the Nuremberg Laws, after Jews had been banned from citizenship, intermarriage, and public schooling. At this late date, there would be no turning back the clock on their total segregation from German society.

Nevertheless, patriotism had apparently beckoned him home on the eve of a war his country had initiated. Even though institutions in the West recognized Gerhart's skills as a political scientist, diplomat, and academic, he couldn't renounce Germany. Rather, he took a job with the Institute for Foreign Policy Research, the Reich's Foreign Office, directing the "America department," where he wrote scholarly essays explaining the historical contexts that had led Germany to war. However, all of his conclusions matched the Reich's official line: he was writing propaganda.

Thus, returning with Mary to the U.S. in 1946, after having both written propaganda and soldiered for the Reich, really wasn't an option, especially for a still-ambitious intellectual. And equally, Mary, after her harrowing years among the Germans, wanted desperately to get home. The prospect of bringing up the children in Germany, a ruined country, must have seemed absurd next to the option of going to America. But perhaps more to the point, surely she felt abandoned by Gerhart, whether for a country or for another woman no one will ever know.

In spite of Mary's evident bitterness towards Gerhart, my mother, Erica, became determined to establish a real relationship with her father. Starting in 1957, Erika began visiting Gerhart. The two of them created a loving relationship, and Mom came to think of Hilde and a half-brother, Dieter, as family.

I have vivid memories of my grandfather, who died when I was nine. He had many of the same traits that I liked in my grandmother. He loved conversation and took children seriously. He would write me illustrated letters with fanciful stories, such as one about an encounter with a sea serpent while fishing. He taught me how to swim in the Mediterranean on a visit to Majorca, and often had wonderful presents for me of beautifully crafted wild animal toys. He and his wife Hilde were sun worshipers, and I remember them as happy, sprightly, and brown under the Majorcan sun.

My mother also visited the Lilienthals in Bonn in the winters of 1957 and '58 and found the same old rapport with them, just as if one year had gone by instead of ten. She also spent several days with Else Wegener and her grown children, Eva and Ernst, as well as her aunt Ilse Jentsch and her family in Bonn.

My Uncle Jerry had a harder time trying to reconnect with his father, finding it hard not to bear a grudge for what he considered Gerhart's abandonment . He writes:

"The fall after we arrived in the United States I entered the second grade and later that year moved to the third. It took a long time to become accepted as a classmate and not seen as a German enemy. What really made me an American was finding an enormous Sears & Roebuck catalog. I spent hours poring over that cornucopia of consumer goods: bicycles with horns, skates, scooters, Silvertone guitars, washing machines, anything. You could even choose the quality you wanted, Good, Better or Best.

"I had everything I needed except a father. For a long time I expected him to join us. I did not see him again until 1964.

"That year I went to Austria with Erika and her husband, David, to see my father and his new family. Erika had much stronger memories of Gerhart. As a child I had been eager to see my father again, but this feeling was mixed with an unconscious resentment, a sense of abandonment. When we met, it was almost as if we were strangers playing the role of father and son. Gerhart had married his former secretary from his Berlin office. Hilde was nice to me, but she didn't speak English, so our conversation was limited. Their son Dieter was like a friendly puppy.

"I was surprised to find that Gerhart and I shared many of the same gestures—and even had a similar sense of humor (we both enjoyed deadpan explanations that start credibly but turn absurd). Gerhart was working for the German Foreign Office in Bonn. He was fluent in English, French, Spanish, and Portuguese and was translating treaty language so that every country involved would have a similar understanding

of what was agreed to.

"I remember asking my father the big question: Why did you leave Switzerland for Germany and how could you have moved to Nazi Germany, where Hitler was exterminating Jews? His answer: 'Germans were unwelcome in Geneva. My parents, my brothers, my home was in Germany. I disagreed with Hitler, and I didn't know the extent of his Jewish policy in 1940. In fact, even in 1945, I had not yet learned about the death camps.' I believe he was telling the truth.

"Gerhart wanted me to stay in Bonn, learn German, get a job or a scholarship, and even bought me a dark blue suit in the then-current German style with large padded shoulders. But after the exuberant Rhineland celebration of Mardi Gras was over, family life in Germany seemed boring and bourgeois to my callow, pot-smoking mind. I was already too unmalleable to become the good German son I might have been. I was eager to travel, so I headed for Italy. I'm sorry to say that I left the suit hanging on a fencepost."

Jerry was drafted early in the Vietnam War, a conflict that he opposed on moral grounds. At Fort Ord he decided to fake psychosis and convinced the army psychiatrists that he wasn't army material. Later he returned to Europe, spending a year with the Living Theater.

Eventually Jerry got a film degree from Boston University and started making a living as a cameraman. He changed his last name from Jentsch to Jones, ostensibly because it made getting jobs easier, but also because, as he put it, "I had no great loyalty to my father." He has a son, Brian, from his first wife, Molly Reagh. He and his wife Delana now split their time between California and an apartment in Berlin. Jerry writes: "Walking one evening at dusk, passing the busy restaurants and lighted shop windows, streetlights painting the Linden trees, and with a vast sky luminous above the spreading city, I felt the stirring of ancient memory, a world familiar to a four- year-old boy on a tricycle."

My mother, Erika, married my Dad, David Mumford, in 1959. Dad became a professor of mathematics at Harvard University, and they lived in Cambridge, Massachusetts, with me and my siblings, Peter, Jeremy, and Suchitra. After my brother and I were born, Mom went back to Radcliffe College to get her Ph.D. in comparative mythology and later became a published and prize-winning poet.

She died of breast cancer in 1988. One of Mom's few real vanities was her hair, which was a luxuriant golden mane that turned silver in middle age. Among all the indignities of cancer and chemotherapy, losing her hair was what she hated the most. Over the years, she told me stories from the trek, but something that particularly stuck with me was her description of sitting outside Vater and Mutter's house in Langenbielau after her bath. She must have been six or seven. Her long, rich, yellow locks were spread around her head and shoulders, drying in the sun, and children walking by would cry out, "Lion, lion!" Mom would smile with pride at the memory.

She sometimes drew on her war-time experiences in her poems, including the one that follows, which was based on the time in Giekau when she and Lütti Lilienthal were sent on a day's journey to a cobbler to get their shoes repaired.

Gerhardt died of a heart attack, dancing at a wedding in the Heidelberg Castle, on August 15, 1970. Mary died two years later, at the age of seventy-three, a continent away.

The Goose-Girl and the Sea

Their clothes were rags.
What did they wear
as war wore on?
A sky-blue silk chemise
That once had been the queen's
is what the goose-girl wore
and loved to wear.
The children all went barefoot.
With tough and dirty feet
they trod upon the stubble, gleaning wheat.

But winter was coming.
They heard a rumor of a shoemaker
still plying his trade in a far town
beside the sea. The two friends begged
and begged to go.

They were given a loaf of bread
a jug of buttermilk and their gaping shoes
packed in their rucksacks.
The boy and girl danced down the road,
she in her mama's slip
he in his missing father's trousers, cut down.
The road unwound
in unfamiliar swoops and curlicues
drawing them on. Never
had they been so far from home.

The soft dust of the road,
the roadside cornflowers as blue as eyes,
the little goose-blossoms, the dandelion suns,
a high hill, breathless climbing slope,
the crest —
before their dazzled eyes
a shimmering surprise
blue in the crystal distance where it flowed
to sky. An aquamarine plenitude, a flood
of wordless joy.
At last
one of them breathed: the sea.

Whether they ever came down from that hill
and found the shoemaker
and stumbled home in darkness
she cannot later tell. But still she sees
— oh sudden prickle of tears behind closed eyes –
the blue, the pure blue of the living sea.

From *Willow Water,* by Erika Mumford;
Every Other Thursday Press (1988)

Chronology

September 26, 1898 – Mary Hunt is born in Louisville, Kentucky.

April 13, 1899 – Gerhart Jentsch is born in Langenbielau, Germany.

1918 – Mary arrives in Boston to attend Simmons College.

1921– She meets Gerhart, who had come to Harvard as a doctoral student in economics.

1926 – Mary sails to France where, on January 26, she marries Gerhart, who, with his friend John Rothschild, runs a student exchange program.

1935 – The couple leave Paris for Geneva, Switzerland; in the same year their daughter, Erika, is born.

1938 – Mary and Gerhart have a son, Jerry.

1940 – In January they leave Geneva for Berlin; Gerhart has taken a job with the Institute for International Research.

1940 – Mary and the children spend the summer with Gerhart's parents in Silesia, missing the first British air raids over Berlin, which took place in August of that year.

1941 – Mary and the children again leave Berlin for Silesia, staying for most of the summer and on through Christmas. In June of that year, after Germany's attack on Russia, Gerhart severs his connection with the Institute and with the Foreign Office. He accepts the chair in American history and civilization at Berlin University's Department of International Affairs. Instead, the University assigns him the task of moving the Department's library to the safety of a 14th-century church in Beeskow. On December 11, Germany declares war on the United States.

1942 – Mary and the children spend much of the year in Berlin, which is under heavy bombardment.

1943 – Under an edict issued by Goebbels, all women with small children, must leave Berlin by August 1 or be evacuated by the government. Unable to find a place to stay in Silesia, Mary takes the children to Pomerania, where she has arranged room and board in Barnimskunow.

Winter of 1943-44 – Friction with the Frau Pastor leads Mary to take a room in the farmhouse of the local estate.

Summer of 1944 – Gerhart, realizing defeat is certain, feels bound to volunteer for the army. He serves first at a divisional radar station on the Eastern Front and then is moved to the front lines. In July the German Army retreats from the East, and civilians in East Prussia begin flight to the West in treks to avoid the approaching Russian troops.

January, 1945 – Mary receives news that Gerhart is fighting in Cosel in Upper Silesia. When months pass with no further word, she believes that he has either been killed or taken prisoner by the Russians.

February 4, 1945 – Mary and the children join the rest of the village of Barnimskunow in its trek to flee enemy troops.

Five days into the journey, Mary and her friend, Dora Lilienthal, take their children and set out on their own.

April-May, 1945 – On April 27, Mary and Dora are taken in by the *Pastorat* in Giekau. On May 8, Germany surrenders.

November 1, 1945 – Mary and the children leave Giekau and take up residence in a refugee camp outside of Bremen, where they await permission to return to America.

December 1945 – Mary learns that Gerhart is alive, though a prisoner of war.

February 10, 1946 – The refugee camp shuts down. Mary and the children move into Bremen, where Mary finds a job and an apartment.

June 27, 1946 – Mary Jentsch and her two children finally return to America.

Ernst-Albrecht (Lütti) Lilienthal drew this picture
for Mary at the start of the Barnimskunow Trek (left to right:
Jerry, Mary, Dora, Lütti, Erika, and Hermann)